BLESSED ARE
THE PEACEMAKERS

BLESSED ARE

THE PEACEMAKERS

A Palestinian Christian
In the Occupied West Bank

Audeh G. Rantisi
with Ralph K. Beebe

Zondervan Books
Zondervan Publishing House
Grand Rapids, Michigan

BLESSED ARE THE PEACEMAKERS
Copyright © 1990 by Audeh G. Rantisi and Ralph K. Beebe

Zondervan Books are published by
Zondervan Publishing House
1415 Lake Drive, S.E.,
Grand Rapids, Michigan 49506

Library of Congress Cataloging-in-Publication Data

Rantisi, Audeh G.
  Blessed are the peacemakers / Audeh G. Rantisi with Ralph K. Beebe.
    p. cm.
  ISBN 0-310-52591-8
    1. Rantisi, Audeh. 2. Palestinian Arabs—West Bank—Biography.
  3. Christians—West Bank—Biography. 4. West Bank—Politics and
  government. I. Beebe, Ralph K., 1932– . II. Title.
  DS110.W47R36 1990
  956.95'30049274—dc20   90–32727
                                                              CIP

Edited by Carol Uridil and Mary McCormick

Printed in the United States of America

90 91 92 93 94 95 / CH / 10 9 8 7 6 5 4 3 2 1

To Pat, our daughters,
and our boys in the Evangelical Home—
in the interest of peace and justice for Palestine

Maps follow page 39
Photos follow page 64

CONTENTS

PREFACE

Audeh and Patricia Rantisi stood with my wife Wanda and me in their West Bank living room in June 1987. We united hands in an intimate circle, praying that God would advance his kingdom through the book we were beginning to write.

A native of the United States, I had never visited the Middle East until after I was fifty. However, my interest in the region began in my childhood. Biblical history has held a special fascination and continuing appeal for me. The God of Abraham, Isaac, and Jacob is the foundation of my life.

As a high school student in 1948 I applauded the rebirth of Israel, and have followed the nation's progress ever since. I saw the fulfillment of biblical prophecy in the historical events. Israel's subsequent agricultural development reminded me of when my father homesteaded farmland in eastern Oregon. Like the heroic Jews ten thousand miles away, he made the desert bloom with luscious, bountiful, irrigated crops.

As a history student and teacher, the Jews interest me. The Nazi holocaust holds a grim fascination, and merits special attention in my classes. I spent one summer at Columbia University, studying New York City's Lower East Side, where a century ago millions of Jews sought refuge from the Czar's cruel pogroms and Europe's vicious anti-Semitism.

Throughout the years I have met many American Jews. One, a colleague named David Curland, profoundly influenced me with his deep insights and human concern.

Until a few years ago, however, I knew little about Palestinian history and knew no Palestinians personally. My entire understanding came from perspectives such as the dust jacket of *The Arab-Israeli Wars*, by Cha'im Herzog: "Israel was born in battle. No sooner had independence been declared than seven Arab armies invaded the tiny, nascent state—bent on its destruction. The tragedy of the Middle East had begun."

I was to learn there is more to the story. My journey to understanding began when Lon Fendall, director of George Fox College's Center for Peace Learning, returned from a trip to the Middle East. He told of a remarkable Palestinian priest named Elias Chacour, and his book, *Blood Brothers*. That book helped me to prepare for my own Middle East study tour in 1986, made possible by the Christian College Consortium.

Our group visited Father Chacour and many other impressive Christian, Moslem, and Jewish educational, religious, and political leaders. Our itinerary included a visit with Audeh Rantisi, a 1948 Palestinian refugee and a victim of Israel's military occupation of the West Bank in 1967.

Reverend Rantisi impressed me. Although ardently nationalistic for the Palestinian cause, he showed concern for the Jews. This melding of political fervor and empathy reminded me of Martin Luther King, Jr., and the nonviolent movement for black rights in the United States.

Palestinians like Chacour and Rantisi opened my heart in a new direction. These apostles of love did not decrease my compassion for the Jews, who remain history's most tragic victims. However, they did help me to understand that the Middle East story has two sides. Sadly, most of the world knows only one.

Like many others, I had stereotyped the Palestinians as "terrorists," failing to recognize that their violence is not unlike that of other human beings. An essential new insight invaded my consciousness, based on these questions: How would I react if the Old Testament revealed that Oregon (my homeland) had been the Jewish Promised Land thousands of years ago? Would I object if they moved in today, took my home, and drove me out?

The television mini-series "Amerika" depicted typical reactions to a Soviet takeover of the United States. Millions of American viewers applauded the patriotic counterviolence—the throwing out of the aggressor. Should I expect less from the Palestinians who lost their homes in 1948 or 1967? The question demands careful analysis.

Audeh Rantisi helped me with that analysis. Therefore, I am pleased to help in shedding light on this man whose life tells the story of Palestinians in a land dominated by Zionist Jews.

The following pages reflect Audeh Rantisi's life and thoughts. He does not have time to go through the process of writing a manuscript and editing, so I did that for him. The organization and wording are mine, and I accept full responsibility.

Wanda and I spent the summer of 1987 on the West Bank, visiting with Audeh and Patricia, taping interviews, reviewing them, then coming together again for clarification and additional questions. I returned for follow-up visits in 1988 and 1989.

Audeh Rantisi and I are indebted to all who helped with this book. Dean Ebner and Douglas Pennoyer, representing the Christian College Consortium's "Internationalizing the Curriculum" program, provided tangible assistance. George Fox College gave me a fully paid one-semester sabbatical. Its academic dean, Lee Nash, offered special encouragement.

Other contributors include Wanda Beebe, who accompanied me in 1987, helped with all the interviews and has been a significant partner in my growth; David and Allison Scott, whose gift helped Wanda to accompany me in 1987; Landrum Bolling, former rector at Jerusalem's Ecumenical Institute for Theological Research (Tantur), whose wisdom and Quaker demeanor proved invaluable during our lengthy stay in 1987; Dan McCracken, manager of Barclay Press, Newberg, Oregon, a great friend and advisor; George Fox College students Jerry Miley, John Hurty, Pam Troyer, Stacy Wright, Michelle Downing, and Laura Engle, who helped the manuscript's progress in many ways; our always helpful secretary Jo Sivley; and most of all, Patricia Rantisi, whose lovely spirit complements Audeh and makes his life complete.

Because Audeh and I regret that the military occupation greatly inhibits educational opportunity, Audeh's half of this book's royalties will fund the education of young people after they leave the Evangelical Home for Boys. My half will assist in providing scholarships for Palestinian students who want to attend George Fox College. As we pray for the peace of Jerusalem, we trust that this book may make a dual contribution: enlightening present readers and educating future leaders of the movement toward a just peace in what should truly be The Holy Land.

> Ralph K. Beebe
> George Fox College
> Newberg, Oregon

FOREWORD

It is ordinary stories, by ordinary people that are "best sellers." The three great Abrahamic stories were set in the Middle East, and have captured the hearts and lives of millions of people across many generations. Although any story after these eternal stories may seem insignificant, Audeh Rantisi has his ordinary yet peculiar story to tell.

In his personal story he tells of the life of every Palestinian. He shares a story of agony, but also of hope. He describes the "postlude" of mutuality, equality, peace, and honoring one another as Jews and as Palestinians.

The story is both a biography and a needed homily. Homilies are not just sermons delivered from the pulpit, but living testimonies of people.

I am happy to introduce this story of an ordinary Christian Palestinian colleague. It is his story. It is my story.

Samir Kafity, S.T.D.
Anglican Bishop in Jerusalem
and President Bishop of
The Episcopal Church
in Jerusalem and the Middle East
26 October, 1988

INTRODUCTION

I am a Palestinian Arab Christian. Born near the Mediterranean coast in Lydda (now renamed Lod), I was eleven when in 1948 the new nation of Israel drove my family from our home to a refugee tent-village in Ramallah, West Bank.

In 1965 my bride and I opened a home for needy boys in Ramallah. Two years later the 1967 war brought Israeli military control to the West Bank. Since then we have experienced the suffocating occupation that in December of 1987 exploded into the *intifada*—our unified attempt to shake off Israeli military occupation of the territories conquered twenty years earlier.

As a boy I pondered John 3:16—about God loving us so much that he gave his Son to die for us—and I accepted Jesus Christ in a personal sense. This religious experience profoundly impacted my life and now sharpens my desire for Palestinian independence and my empathy for my Jewish neighbors. Equally important, I am adamant about finding peaceful solutions to our problems in order to model Jesus the Prince of Peace.

I had many misgivings when several years ago Dan Simmons, then of Mercy Corps International, suggested that I write my life story. Who would want to read about me? Would not people rather learn from a prominent Palestinian with greater political or academic credentials? I still had reservations when Ralph Beebe, a history professor at George Fox College in Oregon, offered to help me with the project.

The world needs to understand the Palestinian story. What better way than through the lives of those who experience firsthand the problems in this crucial region? So I prayerfully decided to tell my story, assured that we could present one man's life in the midst of interesting and enormously significant events.

The Middle East is a complex region with sharp cleavages between Arabs and Jews, and much diversity within both groups. Most Arabs are Moslems, but about ten percent of those in Israel and the occupied territories are Christians. The Moslems are as divergent as Shiites and Sunnis. The Christians are as divergent as Roman Catholics and fundamentalist Protestants. Jews range from ultra-orthodox to atheist, come from disparate cultures throughout the world, and include Caucasians from Europe and blacks from Africa.

A few Jews have lived here for hundreds of years, but most migrated within the last century, as European Zionists led the massive immigration movement that in 1948 became the state of Israel. On the other hand, virtually all Palestinians are native to this area, but most moved or were forced out when the Zionists gained control in 1948–49.

The "Palestinian problem" is this: Zionists and Palestinians claim title to the same property. The Jewish religious-cultural ancestry dates from Abraham four thousand years ago; King David ruled from Jerusalem one thousand years later; after another millennium Rome dispersed the Jews throughout the world.

Following nearly twenty centuries of terrible persecution, many Jews have come to Palestine. Most do not practice Judaism faithfully, and only a few can trace their ancestry to the patriarchs. However, as a culture they strongly identify with the ancients, and have an overwhelming determination to provide their children a fortress against the treacherous world.

Palestinians also look to Abraham as their forefather, basing their primary claim on the right of direct ancestral and personal occupation. Most families can trace their lineage for five hundred years in this land, and many go back more than twice as far.

We suffered a profound shock when in 1948 the Israelis drove us from our homes and made us dependent refugees in our own homeland. Bitter isolation mocked us when most of the world, conscience-smitten by the Nazi holocaust, applauded the eviction. We suffered for Europe's crimes against the Jews. We lost 77 percent of Palestine to Israel as a result of the United Nations' partition and the wars of 1948–49. Israel established military control over the other 23 percent in 1967.

Understandably, most Jews would have preferred to find Palestine completely unpopulated, with no impediment to the founding and occupation of their new homeland. However, many have learned to accept a permanent Palestinian presence. Similarly, most Palestinians would have been glad if the Zionists had never come. Jewish immigration cost us our homes, and for more than four decades has delayed our dreams of independent national status. However, through the years most Palestinians have learned to accept a permanent Israeli presence.

The issue is how to coexist amicably. Israel (the 77 percent of Palestine taken in 1949) contains nearly four million Jews and five hundred thousand Palestinians, the latter living in the Jewish state as citizens, but with reduced rights. In the 23 percent not taken by Israel in 1948–49 (the Gaza Strip and the West Bank, also called the occupied territories), 1.5 million Palestinians have been under Israeli military rule since

1967. Israel controls them with twelve hundred military laws not applicable to the seventy thousand Jews who live there in large apartment-cities called settlements.

This military occupation is the focal point of Palestinian discontent. Israel considers control of the West Bank essential to its own defense (and some Israelis want eventually to annex it into Israel), but Palestinians in the occupied territories seek freedom and fully independent national status.

We must answer this key question: How can we build two independent, secure nations side by side in the land between the Mediterranean Sea and the Jordan River?

First, Israelis must accept Palestine as a nation with the right to choose its own leaders. (Presumably the nation will include the West Bank, Gaza Strip, and East Jerusalem—the 23 percent of Palestine not taken in 1948–49 but occupied by Israel since 1967.)

Second, Palestinians must accept Israel as a nation. Although we might wistfully wish it were not so, Israel enjoys independent, permanent nationhood. We whom Israel evicted in 1948 can never return to our homes.

Despite the dilemma's complexity, the solution depends on mutual acceptance of a simple truth: When these two nations exist side by side, both Palestinians and Jews will enjoy greater security.

I served as Ramallah's deputy mayor for the six years following 1976 (the one time Israel allowed local elections for West Bank Palestinians). However, God's call on my life has led me to the service of my fellow human beings in less political ways. My wife, Patricia, and I run the Evangelical Home for Boys, assist in the associated Evangelical School, and work in our Arab Evangelical Episcopal Church.

We pray that those reading our story will better understand the life of a typical Palestinian—the unique problems of eviction from one's boyhood home, and life under military occupation. We pray that the reader will see God working through his servants and be inspired to help us find peaceful, just solutions to the Middle East problems.

The deepest lesson I have learned in my life is also the simplest: God loves me and others equally. I may dispute what another does, but he or she is not my adversary. I have suffered, but so have others. I do not want Jews to suffer. Down deep where it is important, my Jewish brother and I are very much alike. We have the same need for security and the same need for acceptance. We must learn to provide for each other's security and well-being.

In the spring of 1988 Ted Koppel took his *ABC News Nightline* program to Jerusalem for a week-long report on Palestinian-Israeli problems. The broadcast told a story very familiar to me of another boy whom Zionists drove out of our neighboring town, Ramle. He also had made his way across the mountains and settled in Ramallah.

After growing up, the young man studied law. However, he could never rid himself of the bitter hatred against the Jews who had taken the family home and the land cultivated by his father, grandfather, and many preceding generations. His thirst for revenge involved him in political activities that landed him in prison for many years.

Meanwhile, a Jewish family from eastern Europe took possession of the family house and garden. A little girl was born; when grown, she searched for and found the real owner of her home property. She befriended him and visited him in prison.

Upon her marriage to a rabbi, she lived in Jerusalem. When her parents died, she inherited the house in Ramle. Still conscience-smitten by the injustice of stealing another family's home, she decided to return it to the rightful owner.

At this point the embittered Moslem and the conscientious Jewish woman asked me, a Christian minister, for advice. This moved me deeply—that the Moslem and Jew sought help from a servant of Jesus. We had several meals together and discussed plans to make the house into a school for Arab children because, as the lawyer remarked: "I lost my childhood. I want to help other Palestinian children enjoy theirs."

Unfortunately, our plans never bore fruit. In 1987, Israeli authorities deported the lawyer, adding another layer to his life of tragedy—and showing it starkly as a microcosm of this region.

This poignant story speaks about conscience, human concern, and hope. Most important, it suggests that a loving spirit can break through layers of prejudice and resentment.

In the final analysis Moslems, Jews, and Christians must sit together and discover solutions that will honor all. As a follower of the Prince of Peace, I want to be an agent of reconciliation however possible.

When Ralph Beebe and I began writing, we prayed that this book would glorify God, not any human being. It must simply and briefly report one person's unusual, interesting, instructive experiences—those the world needs to understand. Above all, it must show how much that individual depends on God and praises him for providing the opportunity to serve Christ and fellow human beings. I pray that our effort has been successful.

Audeh G. Rantisi

BLESSED ARE
THE PEACEMAKERS

Death March

I CANNOT forget three horror-filled days in July of 1948. The pain sears my memory, and I cannot rid myself of it no matter how hard I try.

First, Israeli soldiers forced thousands of Palestinians from their homes near the Mediterranean coast, even though some families had lived in the same houses for centuries. (My family had been in the town of Lydda in Palestine at least 1,600 years.) Then, without water, we stumbled into the hills and continued for three deadly days. The Jewish soldiers followed, occasionally shooting over our heads to scare us and keep us moving.

Terror filled my eleven-year-old mind as I wondered what would happen. I remembered overhearing my father and his friends express alarm about recent massacres by Jewish terrorists. Would they kill us, too?

We did not know what to do, except to follow orders and stumble blindly up the rocky hills. I walked hand in hand with my grandfather, who carried our only remaining possessions—a small tin of sugar and some milk for my aunt's two-year-old son, sick with typhoid.

The horror began when Zionist soldiers deceived us into leaving our homes, then would not let us go back, driving us through a small gate just outside Lydda. I remember the scene well: thousands of frightened people being herded like cattle through the narrow opening by armed soldiers firing overhead.

In front of me a cart wobbled toward the gate. Alongside, a lady struggled, carrying her baby, pressed by the crowd. Suddenly, in the jostling of the throngs, the child fell. The mother shrieked in agony as the cart's metal-rimmed wheel ran over her baby's neck. That infant's death was the most awful sight I had ever seen.

Outside the gate the soldiers stopped us and ordered everyone to throw all valuables onto a blanket. One young man and his wife of six weeks, friends of our family, stood near me. He refused to give up his money. Almost casually, the soldier pulled up his rifle and shot the man. He fell, bleeding and dying while his bride screamed and cried. I felt nauseated and sick, my whole body numbed by shock waves. That night I cried, too, as I tried to sleep alongside thousands on the ground. Would I ever see my home again? Would the soldiers kill my loved ones, too?

Early the next morning we heard more shots and sprang up. A bullet just missed me and killed a donkey nearby. Everybody started running as in a stampede. I was terror-stricken when I lost sight of my family, and I frantically searched all day as the crowd moved along.

That second night, after the soldiers let us stop, I wandered among the masses of people, desperately searching and calling. Suddenly in the darkness I heard my father's voice. I shouted out to him. What joy was in me! I had thought I would never see him again. As he and my mother held me close, I knew I could face whatever was necessary.

The next day brought more dreadful experiences. Still branded on my memory is a small child beside the road, sucking the breast of its dead mother. Along the way I saw many stagger and fall. Others lay dead or dying in the scorching midsummer heat. Scores of pregnant women miscarried, and their babies died along the wayside.

The wife of my father's cousin became very thirsty. After a long while she said she could not continue. Soon she slumped down and was dead. Since we could not carry her, we wrapped her in cloth, and after praying, just left her beside a tree. I don't know what happened to her body.

We eventually found a well, but had no way to get water. Some of the men tied a rope around my father's cousin and lowered him down, then pulled him out, and gave us water squeezed from his clothing. The few drops helped, but thirst still tormented me as I marched along in the shadeless, one-hundred-plus degree heat.

We trudged nearly twenty miles up rocky hills, then down into deep valleys, then up again, gradually higher and higher. Finally we found a main road, where some Arabs met us. They took some of us in trucks to Ramallah, ten miles north of Jerusalem. I lived in a refugee tent camp for the next three and one-half years. We later learned that two Jewish families had taken over our family home in Lydda.

Those wretched days and nights in mid-July of 1948 continue as a lifelong nightmare because Zionists took away our home of many centuries. For me and a million other Palestinian Arabs, tragedy had marred our lives forever.

Throughout his life my father remembered and suffered. For thirty-one years before his death in 1979, he kept the large metal key to our house in Lydda.

After more than four decades I still bear the emotional scars of the Zionist invasion. Yet, as an adult, I see what I did not fully understand then: that the Jews are also human beings, themselves driven by fear, victims of history's worst outrages, rabidly, sometimes almost mindlessly searching for security. Lamentably, they have victimized my people.

Four years after our flight from Lydda I dedicated my life to the service of Jesus Christ. Like me and my fellow refugees, Jesus had lived in adverse circumstances, often with only a stone for a pillow. As with his fellow Jews two thousand years ago and the Palestinians today, an outside power controlled his homeland—my homeland. They tortured and killed him in Jerusalem, only ten miles from Ramallah, my new home. He was the victim of terrible indignities. Nevertheless, Jesus prayed on behalf of those who engineered his death, "Father, forgive them . . ."

Can I do less?

Background of the Diaspora

WE ARRIVED in Ramallah when I was eleven, and I lived there for the next seven years. Yet, in my mind Lydda always seemed like home. People in the Middle East experience a strong sense of identity with family, with the land cultivated by their ancestors, and with the house in which they were born and lived. To be torn away so suddenly, without being able even to say good-bye to my personal treasures, left grievous wounds.

When I remember that childhood home, my mind retraces the centuries, wondering about my Christian ancestors. I like to read Acts 9:32–35 with my family in mind:

> As Peter traveled about the country, he went to visit the saints in Lydda. There he found a man named Aeneas, a paralytic who had been bedridden for eight years. "Aeneas," Peter said to him, "Jesus Christ heals you. Get up and take care of your mat." Immediately Aeneas got up. All those who lived in Lydda and Sharon saw him and turned to the Lord.

"All those who lived in Lydda . . ." Maybe my family became Christians that day! According to church records and oral tradition my ancestors lived in Lydda as far back as the fourth century. They could have been there even earlier.

In some ways the history of the Holy Land depresses me. Foreigners have controlled my homeland, often cruelly. Even the Christian crusaders of eight hundred years ago were from the outside. Their treatment of local Christians was deplorable—perhaps no better than their abuse of Jews and Moslems—as they tried to take the Holy Land from the "infidel." However, I do not actually know how those invading armies, those unchristlike Christian crusaders from Europe about 1000 to 1200 A.D., affected my Christian ancestors.

The Ottoman Turks controlled my homeland (and much more of the Middle East) for four hundred years before 1917. The breakup of this empire during World War I brought promise to my grandparents' generation. The Arab world thrilled with hope for independence—an anticipation that, I suppose, was similar to that of the United States in 1776.

During its World War I struggle against the German-Ottoman alliance, Great Britain appealed for and won support from independence-minded Arabs. In return, the British promised to give the Arab people their freedom after the war. The British promised to lend support and help the Arabs establish independent governments.[1] British airplanes dropped leaflets (and the Turkish masters flogged people for picking them up) urging my forbears to "come and join us" who are fighting "for the liberation of all Arabs from Turkish rule so that the Arab Kingdom may again become what it was during the time of your fathers."[2]

My ancestors thought they had won independence when the combined British and Arab troops overthrew the Ottoman Empire. Instead, the British and French betrayed us by extending their own world empires throughout the Middle East. We had merely traded one taskmaster for another. The deception enraged the Arab world, and spawned a continuing mistrust.

Therefore, the freedom movement inched along at a snail's pace. However, Britain and France slowly allowed independence in much of the Middle East. By the end of World War II new nations of Iraq, Jordan, Syria, and Lebanon emerged from the former Ottoman territory. In fact, the entire Middle East was free and independent—except Palestine.

Palestine! My homeland. As a child I understood little, but now I comprehend that we lived in the midst of tragedy. A single word explains our failure to gain freedom: Zionism. Oppressed Jews, called Zionists, were immigrating to Palestine by the hundreds of thousands, hoping to build a new nation in the land that had been Israel three thousand years before. Their presence complicated the Palestinian independence movement; even today we do not have freedom.

Yet I understand the appalling factors that led to the Zionist movement. Zionism is the European Jew's response to centuries of suffering. Jewish history is a litany of horrors—human beings as a group sometimes prohibited from ownership of land, victims of unimaginable inquisitions, pogroms, and finally, concentration camps and gas chambers. The mind cannot comprehend persecution of people merely because they are Semites.

Very early edicts prohibited Christians from socializing with Jews. During the Middle Ages, European nations classified every person as either "Christian" or "Jew"—much to the detriment of the Jews. Several governments expelled all Jews who did not convert to Christianity. (For example, in 1492 Spain allowed its 250,000 Jews three months to convert or leave. Most left.)

The story of Jewish suffering fills volumes. I empathize with them and feel much pain about their suffering. Yet the Palestinians also paid for Europe's atrocities. When the Jews looked for a homeland, many turned to Palestine, the land of their biblical forefathers. Completely ignoring the existence of over one million Palestinians, the Zionists promoted it as "a land without people" just waiting and ready for the Jews, "a people without land."[3] Although the Zionists were mostly secular, nonpracticing Jews, they made profitable, political use of biblical prophecy that suggests an eventual Jewish homeland in Palestine.

During World War I, as Britain and France looked lustfully on the Ottoman Empire while promising the Arabs independence, they also appealed to the Zionists. Wartime agreements with Jewish organizations helped the British fight the war. In 1917 the British foreign secretary, Lord Balfour, informed Zionist organizations that "his Majesty's Government views with favour the establishment in Palestine of a national home for the Jewish people, and will use their best endeavors to facilitate the achievement of this object."[4]

Massive immigration followed. Mid-nineteenth century Palestine was entirely Arab, and only included about twenty-five thousand Jews; a century later over six hundred thousand Jews, nearly all foreigners, comprised nearly one-third of Palestine's population.

For the most part the early immigrant Jews were socialists. They hoped to carve an agrarian, communal society from the land, and live in peace with their Palestinian neighbors. As history's victims, they identified with the underdog.

Yet between the wars, the rapidly immigrating foreign Jews differed from the Arabs and the Arabic-speaking Jews who already lived in Palestine. Although still victims fleeing oppression, many newcomers reflected the materialistic, militant, individualistic Western world—a sharp contrast to the less self-centered, more socially minded, family-oriented Middle East people.

The rapid population increase—the highest rate in the world between the wars[5]—naturally caused problems for the Palestinians. The foreigners, so unlike the Jews who already lived in Palestine, brought disastrous changes. For example, the immigrants forced Palestinians from their jobs, kept them out of trade unions, poured kerosene on their farm crops, and prevented Jewish housewives from shopping in Arab markets (smashing their eggs if they did).[6]

Clashes erupted. By 1936, as local grievances increased and Palestinian nationalistic aspirations languished, large-scale violence raged throughout Palestine. The British army and air force unsuccessfully tried to maintain control, but within three years about 5,000 Arabs, 463 Jews, and 101 British lost their lives.[7] The British developed various potential solutions, but with the outbreak of hostilities in Europe in 1939 they suspended action for the duration of the war.

In the meantime, millions of Jews sought escape from the Nazi holocaust. Most sought admission into Great Britain or the United States, but found extremely tight limitations on Jewish immigration.

Others tried to go to Palestine. However, in 1939 Great Britain, smarting from its inability to maintain control, called for severe limitations on Jewish immigration into Palestine, and an eventual shared Palestinian-Jewish state.

The outraged Zionists, having relied on Britain to help them develop an exclusively Jewish nation, cut the transmission lines and bombed the studio even before the British officially announced the new policy in Palestine.[8] Even though World War II interrupted the plan, the anti-British hostility continued and sometimes erupted into violence. Worldwide sympathy for the Jews undermined Great Britain's ability to act.

One terrorist leader, Menachem Begin (later to become prime minister of Israel), issued a kind of Jewish "declaration of war" against Britain on February 1, 1944, fifteen months before the Allies defeated Hitler. Begin declared:

The time has come to strike against Britain. She herself has written the bloody chapters in the history of Jewish repatriation. Her agents murdered in the towns and in the country. Her judges slandered evilly and went out of their way to dishonour the Jews of the world. . . . There is no longer an armistice between Jewish youth and the British administration in the Land of Israel, which hands our brothers over to Hitler.[9]

Jerusalem's King David Hotel exploded July 22, 1946. Begin's performance killed more than eighty people—including British, Jewish, and Arab. Although most Jews joined the rest of the world in revulsion, such acts, along with pro-Zionist political pressure from the United States, influenced the British to concede. They finally threw the situation to the United Nations, which in 1947 decided to partition Palestine into two separate nations—one for Arabs and one for Jews. The immigrants received more than half of the Palestinian land, although the Jews owned less than eight percent at that time. Thus, Palestine became available to even more Zionists—a chilling prospect for Palestinians already inundated with immigrant Jews.

The British (and the rest of the world) forgot—actually, ignored—the final phrase of Lord Balfour's 1917 declaration in which he said Britain would move toward a Jewish homeland: ". . . it being clearly understood that nothing shall be done which may prejudice the civil and religious rights of the existing non-Jewish communities in Palestine."[10]

Unquestionably, the results did "prejudice the civil and religious rights" of the Palestinian people. A Zionist state soon became a nightmare. In addition, the United Nations disdained the other half of its partition promise: While putting much energy into the birth and support of Israel, it did nothing to encourage the creation of an independent Palestinian state.

Although only a child at the time, I remember many of the events of 1948. I had had Jewish friends all my life, and there had been no animosity. Most Arabs and Jews had lived peacefully for centuries in neighboring towns and countries. No one interfered with the other's religion. Most were Moslem, a few Jewish, some Christian, and for the most part, all coexisted in peace and neighborliness.

Then everything changed. The crusading European Zionists threatened the security of the nations emerging from European control, including Lebanon, Syria, Jordan, Iraq, Egypt, and Saudi Arabia. Aggressive, arrogant, intolerant of Christians and Moslems, the Europeanized immigrant Jews menaced those around them.

After victory over the British, the Zionists turned their attention to the Palestinians, who still impeded their progress. They wanted total control of the land the United Nations had given them, and they sought potential expansion beyond that. They intended to drive the impediment from the land.

The aggressors attacked throughout Palestine. Not content to merely evacuate the land mandated to the Jews, they also assaulted villages that the United Nations had reserved for the Palestinians. They even attacked the Jerusalem International Zone.

One informed researcher, David K. Shipler, writes of Zionism's "anti-Arab bigotry, religious zealotry, Jewish terrorism, and . . . affinity for violence," and points out that since 1948 Israelis have taught their children an "official myth" regarding our flight from our homes: that we left willingly, not wishing to live in a Jewish state, and that, expecting a quick victory that would allow the Palestinians to return home almost immediately, the Arab Legion ordered us out.

Shipler notes that this myth—that Jews had no responsibility for our flight—is flawed. True, some Palestinians did leave their homes to escape the fighting, as in any war. Others probably responded to the Arab Legion's warnings, and a few went to Beirut or Amman, expecting a quick return when the fighting ended. Many others, however,

> were deliberately and forcibly expelled by the Jews. And others fled because they were convinced that if the Jews got into their villages, they would massacre men, women, and children as they had done in the village of Deir Yassin in April, 1948, one month before Israel became a state.[11]

As a boy I felt my parents' fear of the warlike, barbaric Zionists. We learned about Deir Yassin, an Arab village outside Jerusalem, in the spring of 1948. Six weeks before Israel became a nation, Zionist terrorists killed at least 250 people there. They intended to intimidate and scare all Palestinians. I will let a witness, Meir Pa'il, a Jewish intelligence officer, tell his observations of what happened:

> It was a massacre in hot blood; it was not preplanned. It was an outburst from below with no one to control it. Groups of men went from house to house looting and shooting, shooting and looting. From within the houses you could hear the cries of Arab women, Arab elders, Arab kids. I tried to find the commanders, but I did not succeed. I tried to shout and to hold them, but they took no notice. Their eyes were glazed. It was as if they were drugged, mentally poisoned, in ecstasy.[12]

Although not present at the time, Menachem Begin responded with this message to his compatriots:

> Accept my congratulations on this splendid act of conquest. . . . We are all proud of the excellent leadership and the fighting spirit in this great attack. . . . Tell the soldiers: You have made history in Israel with your attack and your conquest. Continue this until victory. As in Deir Yassin, so

everywhere, we will attack and smite the enemy. God, God, Thou has chosen us for conquest.[13]

In his memoirs Begin notes that: "Out of evil, . . . good came," and applauds the terror it caused, because fear of becoming another Deir Yassin made "evacuation" of other Arab villages (including Lydda) much easier.[14] After the massacre he sent messengers to nearby Arab towns and villages to announce that the Jews were coming.

Israel officially became a nation May 14, 1948. In the several months immediately before and after that date Zionists destroyed about eighty percent of all Palestinian villages and towns—more than 350 in all. One Jewish observer recalled later:

> We old Jewish settlers in Palestine who witnessed the fight could tell . . . how and in what manner we, Jews, forced the Arabs to leave cities and villages. . . . Some of them were driven out by force of arms; others were made to leave by deceit, lying and false promises. It is enough to cite the cities of Jaffa, Lydda, Ramle, Beersheba, Acre from among numberless others.[15]

Fearful for their own security, the newly independent Arab nations decided to resist. They had good reason: Some Zionists had vowed to eventually occupy everything from the Nile in Egypt to the Euphrates in Iraq. Further, Zionism continued and extended European imperialism at a time when the Middle Eastern nations resolved to throw off centuries of outside control. So a war of Middle East self-defense lasted for more than a year. In the end the poorly armed Arabs lost the war and all but twenty-three percent of Palestine.

Noting that pro-Israel historians have convinced the world that the Arab nations attacked Israel, Professor Sami Hadawi argues:

It was only after British withdrawal, and immediately follow-ing proclamation of the state of Israel on 14 May 1948, that the Arab armies entered Palestine soil. But much had already happened in the country which called for intervention by the Arab states.

If as a result of this intervention the Arab states are to be regarded as the aggressors, then, according to this logic, it would be difficult to defend the British and French declaration of war on Nazi Germany in 1939 as an action undertaken to protect and uphold human rights, liberty, and freedom. It is what *really* took place before the two opposing armies faced each other on the battlefield that must fix responsibility for the war.

Just as the Allied Powers could no longer tolerate Nazi aggression, so the Arab States could not allow their defenseless kinsmen in Palestine to be massacred, ill-treated, and ousted from their ancestral homeland without raising a helping hand. In fact, the Arab States must be regarded to have taken it upon themselves to carry out the responsibilities of the United Nations, which had guaranteed to protect the rights, property, and interests of the minorities in a partitioned Palestine.[16]

The Israelis attacked Lydda in July of 1948—one of the new nation's earliest aggressive actions against the part of Palestine not given to them by the United Nations. The Israeli military subjected us to air raids by night and shelling by day; then the soldiers came. Historians Jon and David Kimche describe the invasion, in which Moshe Dayan, commanding the 89th Jeep Commando force, "drove at full speed into Lydda, shooting up the town and creating confusion and a degree of terror among the population." On July 11, Lydda's "Arab population of 30,000 either fled or were herded on to the road to Ramallah. The next day Ramle also surrendered, and its Arab population suffered the same fate. Both towns were sacked by the victorious Israelis."[17]

The conquest of Lydda was not a repeat of Deir Yassin; rather, the soldiers tricked us into assembling at the church, making us think it was just a search, as the British did when they controlled Palestine. However, when we tried to return home later that day soldiers filled the streets; they ordered us away, through that narrow gate and into the mountains. About one hundred thousand Palestinians in Lydda and nearby towns lost their homes at the same time. Some estimate that four thousand died from thirst and exhaustion during our three-day march.

Ethel Mannin uses our story as the setting of her novel, *The Road to Beersheba.* Her accurate description of our exodus stirs my memory:

> The temperature in the coastal plain was over a hundred in the shade—the thin shade of the olive trees, the red shade of the rocks. Only the compulsion of terror made it possible to walk in that heat, over that terrain. Israeli troops drove the people off the roads and deeper into the wilderness, deeper into the endless bare hills.
>
> The earth was made of sand too hot to be touched by the naked foot; it was made of sand and stones and grey boulders and clumps of bleached thorn. It was undulating land, flowing away to the hills, which fold upon fold, melted into a sky heat-drained of all colour. The landscape was vast, flowing away to infinity in all directions, the vast Jordanian wilderness, teeming now with people, mostly women and children, like a scattered army, stumbling over the stones, picking a way through the boulders, toiling up the sandy hillocks, drenched with sweat, stumbling, falling, rising and stumbling on again, women clutching babies, dragging old people, and the old collapsing and unable to rise again. But always the onward surge of people, driven by fear, stumbling on urgently through the blinding sunlight, placing one foot before the other among the stones, because not to do so was to die, of sunstroke, or thirst, or exhaustion.

And always was the fear of the small black civilian planes, coming in low, so low you could see the men in them hovering and swooping like birds of prey, as they had come in that last terrifying night in Lydda. . . .

They were all making for the little hill town of Ramallah, a few miles from Jerusalem, but driven far out into the wilderness, the road no longer in sight, only a few of the younger ones had any real sense of direction. The rest walked blindly eastward; all that mattered was that Lydda should be behind them.[18]

We who fled to Ramallah did not suffer alone. Of about 1.3 million Arabs who lived in Palestine in 1948, between seven hundred thousand and nine hundred thousand lost their homes—some of us forcefully driven out, others fleeing to escape the invaders. Historian Donald Neff tells it like it was:

While Jews, many of them recently arrived from Europe, moved into the houses that Palestinians had lived in for generations, and in some cases for centuries, the displaced Palestinians huddled in crude refugee camps, homeless, landless, and filled with hatred.[19]

Another historian, David Hirst, tells of the Zionists' conquests even more graphically:

They came into possession of entire cities, or entire quarters of them, and hundreds of villages. All that was in them—farms and factories, animals and machinery, fine houses and furniture, carpets, clothes, and works of art, all the goods and chattel, all the treasured family heirlooms of an ancient people—was theirs for the taking. Ten thousand shops, businesses, stores and most of the rich Arab citrus holdings—half the country's total—fell into their hands.[20]

Relating the twentieth-century history of my people makes the Zionists seem cruel and inhuman. Sometimes they were. Yet, I must always remember that they are human beings just like the rest of us, loved by God no less, and subject to the same needs for security and acceptance. Their actions stem from a tragic history of victimization resulting, they claim, in a God-given mandate to make things right in their own eyes. Primarily agnostics or atheists, they only use religion as a cover for their political purposes. Most Zionists are much different from the small minority of devout Orthodox Jews. Yet I believe that we must always show them love, even though we hate the cruelty and racism they practice.

The events of 1948 destroyed my world. Overnight I became a homeless, dependent refugee. Nevertheless, with the resiliency of youth and a life-changing personal encounter with God, I found purpose and meaning in life. As I grew older, an unyielding determination to serve Jesus Christ, my Lord, nudged me toward a life of love, service, and peaceful support of my father and grandfather's dream of a free Palestine.

I lived in Ramallah for the next seven years. During that period I made decisions that set the course of my entire life. Gradually the bitterness began to erode; however, the process was not easy.

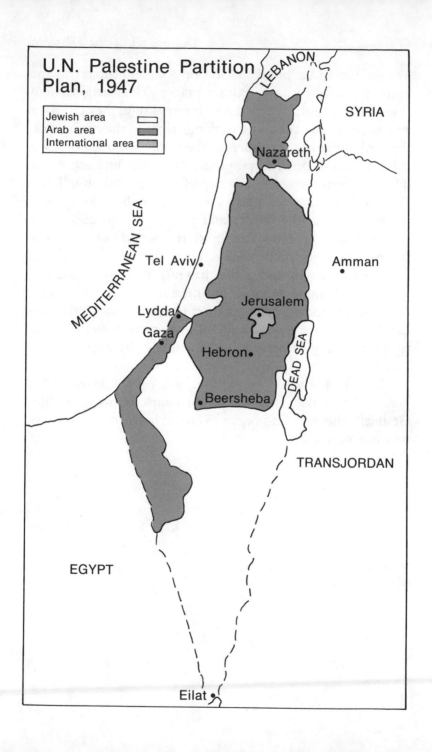

U.N. Palestine Partition
Plan, 1947

Jewish area
Arab area
International area

LEBANON
SYRIA

MEDITERRANEAN SEA

Nazareth

Tel Aviv

Amman

Lydda

Jerusalem

Gaza

Hebron

DEAD SEA

Beersheba

TRANSJORDAN

EGYPT

Eilat

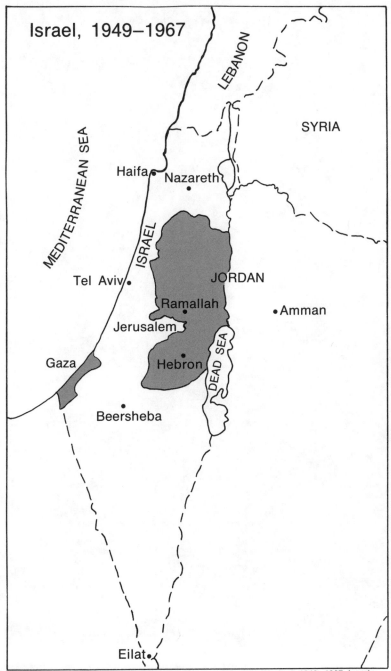

Israel, 1949–1967

MEDITERRANEAN SEA

LEBANON

SYRIA

Haifa

Nazareth

ISRAEL

Tel Aviv

JORDAN

Ramallah

Amman

Jerusalem

Gaza

DEAD SEA

Hebron

Beersheba

Eilat

The Gaza Strip was a part of Egypt and West Bank a part of Jordan from 1949–1967. Israel took military control of these lands in 1967.

From Despair to Hope

*I*N *LYDDA* my family lived in a large house, with sixteen centuries of tradition, our olive oil soapmaking business, and positive self-esteem.

In Ramallah we lived in a tiny tent, with no local roots, no way of making a living, and a constant sense of worthlessness.

Thousands staggered into Ramallah that July, homeless and destitute. The thirteen surviving members of my family arrived possessionless, carrying nothing but the tattered clothing we wore. Altogether, more than seven hundred thousand refugees migrated to the West Bank, Gaza, the Arab Middle East, and the United States. About three hundred thousand Arabs remained in Israel, living as second-class citizens in a nation controlled by the aggressors.

Ethel Mannin describes the scene in Ramallah precisely as I remember it:

> Even before the arrival of the main body of refugees, from Lydda and Ramleh, the little hill town presented an astonishing sight, with the thousands of homeless milling in its narrow main street looking for food and shelter. Under every olive tree on the hillside terraces a family was camped out, and in every garden and along every wall and fence of the pine-flanked avenues of the residential quarter, primitive tents of sacking, even portions of clothing, were rigged up, to shelter men, women, and children, providing them with an illusion of privacy and a home. . . .

Ramallah received the first impact of that major human disaster. It reeled under the impact, but recovered from the shock and began to organize; army lorries from Amman, far away on the arid hills at the other side of the Great Jordan Valley, came rumbling in laden with sacks of flour. Loud speakers in the streets directed the people to distribution centres. The big American Friends Boys' School was immediately turned into a temporary hospital and clinic for the sick and wounded of the terrible exodus and for the babies born during it, and their exhausted mothers.

The people ravaged the olive groves and orchards and vineyards for wood for their fires, and the owners winced but brought traditional Arab hospitality to bear. "Tfadalu," they said. "Help yourselves!" How should the starving and destitute and homeless be denied? The nations of the world had voted away their country to the Jews, and the Jews had entered into possession of their homes and lands. God have mercy on their homelessness and hunger. Such as we have, we give them. Tfadalu.[1]

My memories parallel Ethel Mannin's research: Upon arriving in Ramallah, we discovered many helpful people, even though the flood of refugees had severely disrupted the community both economically and socially.

I will always remember the graciousness of Joseph Tannous and others at the Friends (Quaker) Girls' School. They met us and offered a place to stay temporarily. Although thousands lived under the trees, we happened to be among those who occupied the school during the balance of the summer recess.

Every classroom held five families, one in each corner and one in the middle; another lived on the landing halfway up the stairs. My extended family, a total of thirteen, shared one corner.

We were miserable. Waves of resentment aggravated our helplessness. I was homesick. I could not understand what had happened. Why had the United Nations given my country to the Jews? Why had it let the Jews take my home?

One day Count Folke Bernadotte, a special envoy from the United Nations who was trying to make peace, came to our refugee camp. He recorded this in his diary:

> Never have I seen a more ghastly sight than that which met my eyes here at Ramallah. The car was literally stormed by excited masses shouting with Oriental fervour that they wanted food and wanted to return to their homes. There were plenty of frightening faces in that sea of suffering humanity. I remember not least a group of scabby and helpless old men with tangled beards who thrust their emaciated faces into the car and held out scraps of bread that would certainly have been considered uneatable by ordinary people, but was their only food.[2]

Perhaps my grandfather was one of those "scabby and helpless" old men, ashamed that he could no longer care for his family. Very likely he was. Touched by the suffering, Count Bernadotte expressed concern about the refugee problem, Israel's expanding military power, and the Zionists' "large scale looting, pillaging, and plundering." He added:

> It would be an offense against the principle of elemental justice if these innocent victims of the conflict were denied the right of return to their homes while Jewish immigrants flow into Palestine, and indeed, at least offer the threat of permanent replacement of the Arab refugees who have been rooted in the land for centuries.
> ... the liability of the Provisional Government of Israel to restore private property to its Arab owners and to indemnify those owners for property wantonly destroyed is clear.[3]

I am grateful that Count Bernadotte tried to bring justice. However, injustice prevailed. A few days later Zionist terrorists assassinated Bernadotte near Mandelbaum Gate in Jerusalem.[4]

Classes resumed at the Friends Girls' School in September, the Red Cross gave us a tent that was about four meters (thirteen feet) square, and we joined the thousands outside. The Red Cross also provided a minimum supply of blankets and clothing, and periodically, flour for bread, and a little milk for the babies.

Our situation was neither pleasant nor healthy. For bathroom needs the thirteen of us shared a tin can, or walked beyond the edge of the camp. We had no furniture, except a small kerosene stove we used outside the tent for cooking bread.

In spite of everything, my family tried to maintain its traditions. Many refugees and nearly all the residents of Ramallah were Christians. The name "Ram Allah" means *Hill of God* in Arabic.

While living in the tent-camp, I sometimes pondered familiar Bible stories as I walked the two miles to fetch water at the spring. It was not far from the place where Joseph and Mary discovered that twelve-year-old Jesus was missing (Luke 2:41–50). That night Mary and Joseph probably used a similar spring in Ramallah. In pondering such matters as the importance of watering places in the Old Testament, I often found pleasure in daydreaming about the heroes of the faith of my fathers.

We shivered through a cold first winter in the tent. About three thousand feet above sea level, Ramallah sharply contrasted with our warm sea-level home in Lydda. It snowed. At first I delighted in the white flakes—a new experience for me—but the cold and snow brought tragedy. Many people died of disease from exposure and lack of good food.

My sister slipped and fell in the snow, breaking her arm. As she suffered, the tiny tent seemed to shrink. With the snow came periods of rain. Water entered our floorless tent, flooding us, making it almost as wet inside as out. My life consisted of cold, hunger, and misery. I dreamed of home and hated the Zionists.

Meanwhile, the war between Israel and the Arab nations continued, finally ending in 1949. Israel controlled 77 percent of Palestine instead of the 57 percent mandated by the United Nations. In defiance of the U.N., Israel made Jerusalem its capital. The next year Jordan officially occupied the West Bank (which included Ramallah) and Egypt controlled the Gaza Strip. The League of Arab States and the United Nations opposed these annexations, but neither Jordan nor Egypt relinquished control, and we did not gain independence.[5] Once again we fell under another nation's control. Although the Jordanians were Arabs, they seemed little improvement over the British who had ruled since World War I.

However, with life merely an attempt to survive from day to day, the political situation had lost its significance. The hope that we could return home faded and began to die. Despair followed.

We had to live, but had no money. I sold cigarettes, kerosene, and little cakes my mother made. I distributed kerosene around the tent-camp, carrying the jars on my shoulders. Later I worked in a coffee shop in Ramallah.

I have often wondered how my parents withstood the sadness of those terrible years. For most Middle Easterners life is synonymous with family. Family is near and distant kinship, love, and a house where one's ancestors have faced the hardships of life together. I know the sudden convulsion in July of 1948 damaged my parents more deeply than they let us see.

Yet bravely and stoically they clung to the important things. My mother knew hardship long bfore our exodus to

Ramallah. She had lost both parents to a plague when she was a little girl. A very devout Christian woman, she regularly took me to church before we lost our home. Her wonderful prayer life pointed me toward God's love and his purposes for my life. In later years she felt so close to heaven that she conversed aloud with God. She said she could hear the angels singing. I owe much to her relationship with God and to her devout prayers.

My father was also religious, but much less expressive. He was unable to read, but was politically astute. He wondered why most of the world, particularly the United States and Great Britain, condoned and even applauded everything Israel did to the Palestinians. He could not understand why the Christians there just stood by and let it happen. He anguished over this injustice for the last half of his life. He provided a wise model for me with his criticism of the source of our adversity, yet his stoic recognition that we must live within the limitations of reality.

In some ways my parents' loving concern overrode the hopelessness of the tent village, and enabled my mind to remain active. I thought a lot about what had happened and what might be ahead. I particularly remember pondering the future: What is this life? Surely there must be something more. I should try to do something with my life that will mean more than merely existing in this tent. Yet the options seemed extremely limited for a Palestinian teenager torn from family roots and land.

During noon hours and after work I helped out in the carpentry shop next door. I began to learn the trade. As Jesus must have done, I enjoyed the smell of the wood, the feel of becoming a craftsman, and the sense of self-worth. I had something to replace my father and grandfather's despair and loss of self-respect caused by their inability to provide for our family. I worked there eighteen months.

Then in 1951, when I was fifteen, opportunity unfolded. Carl Agerstrand, a dedicated Lutheran layman from Muskegon, Michigan, sold his business and gave the money to open a boarding school for Palestinians. He called it "The Home of the Sons."

My mother delighted me when she asked if I wanted to go to school. I welcomed the chance to attend. After three and one-half years without education, I quickly applied and was the first person accepted.

Freedom from the refugee camp at last! I was going to school! The teachers did not require an entire year in a single grade and allowed me to study hard and catch up. By age eighteen I had finished high school.

In broken Arabic, Carl Agerstrand constantly counseled: "Remember John 3:16." At first I did not understand exactly what he meant; however, I often read the verse. Then one day in 1952, the words literally leaped from the page and the Word of God came alive in my heart: "For God so loved the world, that he gave his only begotten Son, that whosoever believeth in him should not perish, but have everlasting life" (KJV).

What a verse! That God's son had died for my sins, had forgiven me and made me his child, finally struck home with life-changing clarity. How profoundly it influenced me! I accepted the message of love at face value and surrendered my life to Jesus Christ. Sustained by his love, I found that the power of his cross and resurrection gave purpose to my life. Committed to his will, I have tried to be a faithful servant in the succeeding decades.

Many religions exist, but there is only one Savior, Jesus Christ. My ancestors had been Christian for many centuries, but this experience was personal. He died for me personally. I accepted him personally, and I will never again be the same.

This conversion experience did not decrease my passion for a national homeland. In some ways acceptance of God's teaching increased my concern for justice and sharpened my Palestinian nationalism. It helped me know that while hating what the Zionists did, I could love them as human beings. I pray that they find will find the true Messiah, and stop their exploitation. The love is real—I really do seek to understand the reasons for what they do, and sympathize with their insecurities.

The paradox is fascinating: The spiritual experience heightened my disgust for injustice but increased my understanding of its causes and my empathy for its perpetrators. All of us are capable of inflicting terrible indignities; all of us can find forgiveness and redemption in the power of God's love.

Two years later, as I was rereading John 3:16, the Lord spoke to me again about my future life and what I might do with it. "For God so loved the world that he gave his only begotten son, that whosoever . . ." *Whosoever!* That meant not only me, but the rest of the world. Did God want me to influence others to accept the truth of his gospel? Did he want me to give my life's ambition to him and merely follow where he led? Did he want to lead me into any special ministry? I clearly remember walking one Sunday afternoon, thinking and praying. I stopped, bowed my head, closed my eyes, and promised: "Lord, you will be my guide." What a sense of peace filled me! I turned my entire life to God's direction, come what may.

By then, Robert Grupp, who came to direct the Home of the Sons in 1952, was the primary human instrument in my life. As my mentor he influenced me more than any other person. He led his students in an intensive study of the book of Isaiah and other sections of the Bible. We memorized the book of John, many Psalms, 1 Corinthians 13, the Christmas story, and the story of the Crucifixion. As I grew older, I realized that the memorized text is less important than the broader meaning of Scripture, but I learned much while committing it to memory, and still remember a lot—a real benefit.

Even today I still thank God for Bob Grupp's dedicated influence. He was committed to the needs of boys in a country far from his homeland. A man of principles, a good mentor, friend, administrator, and pastor—his life still inspires me.

A period of profound searching accompanied my intensive scriptural study and second spiritual awakening. I felt a tugging toward more education and a different life although, as the oldest son, my family needed me. Should I stay in Ramallah and work either as a carpenter or in the olive oil soapmaking business my family was trying to develop? Or should I try to find a place to go to school? Was the Lord calling me to additional training in a more specialized Christian ministry?

In 1955 I heard about the Bible College of Wales. My heart hungered to learn more of God's biblical truth. I desperately wanted to go. After much prayer I wrote, received the admission forms, filled them out, and returned them. Several anxious days later a letter came from Swansea. They had accepted me!

But I had no money. How could I go? Was it all boyish foolishness—wishful thinking? The supreme lesson of my life followed: I must completely trust in Jesus' power. He will provide the means if he wants me to have my desire. If he does not, he will change my desire to correlate with his will.

chapter three

I continued to pray, knowing that we still have him even when we think we have nothing. As the school's enrollment deadline neared, I bargained with God: "God, you know how much I want to go. You also know how much I want to do your perfect will. Please, if you want me in school, tomorrow morning you send me the money. If the money doesn't come tomorrow, I really won't mind, because I will understand that you want me here."

Nervously I checked the morning's mail. In it was an envelope that contained enough money for me and two others to go to Swansea. I still do not know who sent that envelope, but I know that God does.

A few days later, in October of 1955, three Palestinian Arabs—Naim Nassar, Elias Asi, Audeh Rantisi—embarked into the unknown, the greatest adventure of our young lives. As we left Ramallah, I had little idea what the future would bring. But like the hymn writer, I did know who holds tomorrow, and I knew he held my hand.[6]

chapter four

A New Life

E *MOTION* overflowed as we left our families in
October of 1955. I had lived in Lydda, Ramallah, and
nearby communities for eighteen years. Yet, buoyant anticipation of our adventure overpowered the loneliness.

We took public transportation to Amman, then Damascus
and Beirut. From there we boarded a Turkish ship that
steamed into the Mediterranean, moving slowly past Cyprus
and Crete, and on to Marseilles on the southern coast of
France. We disembarked, quickly boarded a train for Paris,
and then went on to Calais. From there we traveled across the
English Channel to Dover and London, and concluded with a
bus ride to Swansea in South Wales. The entire trip was a
cultural feast for a young man with no experience beyond his
immediate surroundings.

We alighted as the rainy evening in Swansea closed around
us. Our first stop was the dining room for a dinner of fried
tomatoes with a poached egg, a piece of toast, and a cup of
tea—an unfamiliar diet for young Palestinians. And we were
on display: While we ate, many eyes peeked into the room,
wondering at their first sight of Arabs. I can assure you that
the curiosity was mutual.

As the weeks went by, I became lonely. Two thousand
miles is a long way from family and friends. The cultural
distances were even greater. Yet, the students and staff of the

Bible College of Wales were open and accepting. More importantly, I felt Jesus' continued presence in my life, and was sure that I remained in his will. While at Swansea I learned to put myself on the line for God—trusting that he had a purpose for me and that I could follow it. Often I had to depend directly on God, even for small things.

One day I received an important letter with a request for an immediate response. As usual I had no money, not even enough for a stamp. I went ahead and wrote the answer, then asked the Lord what to do next, and thanked him in faith. I went outside, toward the post office—and found an unused two pence half-penny stamp in the street. After mailing the letter, I went to my room and thanked God.

While furthering my education at the Bible college, I felt God calling me to preach his Word. One Wednesday someone asked me to go to another town and give the next Sunday's sermon. While preparing, I prayed about transportation, knowing I would have to exercise total faith. Sure that the Lord wanted me to go, I reasoned that he would get me there. On Sunday morning I arose early enough to catch the first bus. Still penniless, I prayed, "Lord, you are able. Show me your Word, please. Give me something from your book."

I turned to Psalm 34 and read it all, including:

> I sought the Lord, and he heard me, and delivered me from all my fears. . . . This poor man cried, and the Lord heard him, and saved him out of all his troubles. . . . The Lord is nigh unto them that are of a broken heart; and saveth such as be of a contrite spirit (KJV).

With a "Thank you, Lord," I arose from my knees, washed, dressed, went to the station, and got on the bus. A man with a Bible sat beside me with a cheery "Good morning, brother!" He asked where I was going. I told him, and we talked about my life and the Lord's work. Then I saw the conductor coming to collect money for our tickets.

I had said nothing about my finances, but as the conductor approached, the man beside me put his hand on mine and, reaching into his own pocket, drew out enough for his ticket and mine, and even more—he also bought me a return ticket. I could not argue with his generosity, so I graciously accepted. He never knew that God had used him to answer a prayer.

Life at Swansea continued to be a series of similar miracles. I waited in dependence upon God, realizing that he wanted me there and would not fail. The college provided a challenging academic climate. Classes were superb. I loved to learn! Joy welled up in my soul as I experienced excellent teaching, studied the Word, and tried to practice a life of obedience.

The college radiated a missionary concern for God's work to be accomplished throughout the world. Students and faculty enjoyed long prayer meetings, sometimes from supper until after midnight.

Each teacher left a positive impression on my life. Three stand out especially. One was the Rev. Ieuan Jones, a Welshman, a splendid New Testament and Christian doctrine teacher whose lectures were so fascinating that sometimes I completely forgot where I was. Another was Dr. Kenneth Symonds, who taught Bible characters and elementary medicine. The third was the Rev. Samuel Howells, who taught church history. These godly men provided me with joyful blessings because they knew so much and committed their lives so fully to Christ. All three spent much time in prayer. Therein lay their secret.

The Bible College of Wales was coeducational. Naturally, some interesting young ladies crossed my pathway. I liked especially an outstanding and personable English girl named Patricia Greening. Often she generously loaned me her bicycle. I made sure to keep air in the tires, and did favors for her whenever possible. However, since the school believed that close relationships were detrimental to its goal of preparing missionaries, dating was prohibited. So we did not go out, except once when Patricia's mother visited. I took advantage of her presence to arrange a long three-person walk on the beach, and ended it with a cup of tea. I remember asserting in that little cafe: "Patricia, one day you will come to my country." She just laughed, doubting that would ever happen.

The school offered few opportunities for political discussions or involvement. The subject was not prohibited, but there were no natural outlets. My stomach would grind with frustration from the ardent pro-Israel, anti-Arab stance in the newspapers and the attitudes that surrounded me. I suffered from being so completely, albeit quietly, at odds with British public opinion during the Suez crisis in October 1956. Most people just did not understand.

Those Christians at Swansea were wonderful and missionary minded, but knew little about the victims of European imperialism. Christian speakers shared inspiring missionary messages but displayed grave ignorance of the native people's perspectives. Like many of today's evangelicals, most had one outlook on the Middle East, and that was pro-Israel. They were totally pro-Western—as out of touch with Palestinian reality as the Zionists.

Only four Arabs attended the college (the three Palestinians and one Lebanese). We privately shared our concerns, but disclosed them to few others. At times we wanted to speak out, to tell the other side of the story, but we did not want to cause problems.

Three years sped by and I was a Bible college graduate. Returning to Ramallah in 1958, I frequently visited The Home of the Sons where I had once lived. By then, Donald Ohman ran it. I learned later that he hoped and prayed that if God's will indicated, I would ask about a position there. Meanwhile, I prayed that if God wanted me to work there, Mr. Ohman would ask me. God soon revealed to us each other's prayers. For two years I served boys who reminded me of myself a decade earlier.

Donald Ohman suffered from severe hay fever, so I managed the school during his frequent incapacities. Modeling Bob Grupp, I emphasized Bible study and memorization of God's Word. I conducted church services, sports programs, and field trips. These were meaningful, fulfilling years that allowed me to serve as I had been served. At one point I felt we should have a Christian school, and prayed that God would send someone for that purpose. I discovered that God's response to my prayer request was: How about you?

I felt the Lord leading me toward further education, in order to qualify for greater service in Ramallah. I believed that I needed a more complete, well-rounded understanding of the world—training in the liberal arts. God seemed to be calling me to minister his Word. I needed to speak biblical truth with an empathetic human understanding. I needed answers to important questions: Why is the world like it is? What are the lessons of history? What can we do to bring change? How might I best contribute?

Then, in the spring of 1960, Robert Grupp, who had returned to the United States and was pastoring the First Presbyterian Church in Aurora, Illinois, contacted me about furthering my education. He thought his congregation might bring me to Aurora College, so he "put out a fleece." After telling the people about me, they prayed and took a Sunday evening offering. They decided they would invite me to attend the school if a certain amount came in. The congregation gave double the amount needed. Once again I was off to a far land in search of additional understanding.

Bob Grupp later explained the process that brought me to Aurora:

> I maintained contact with Audeh after I returned to the United States and became a pastor at Aurora. The congregation at the First Presbyterian Church was very missions-oriented, and always expressed interest in my experiences in the Holy Land. In 1960 I became burdened that Audeh have an opportunity for further education, so I approached the people, recommending that we completely finance his education, including transportation and spending money.
>
> Other than raising the money, the only concern was the possibility that he would not return home. The congregation decided however, that that would be between him and the Lord. We should not attempt to control his life, but supply him the opportunity to become educated, without strings attached. I felt confident that Audeh would return home, but felt his place of service should be up to him and the Lord. If possible, we should give him an opportunity. So we took an offering that brought in double the needed amount! In reality, Audeh was not the only beneficiary of this church's generosity: We made him a pastoral assistant and so we were able to learn from him, too.

The people at Aurora College and the Presbyterian Church were genuine, caring, and helpful. I felt completely at home, experiencing the beauty of a fraternal relationship with others in the body of Jesus Christ.

I love the Dietrich family—Leslie, Ruth, and Tom—who adopted me into their home and became my warm, caring family. I felt both free and welcome there. It was a good feeling, much like the feeling one has in the close extended families of the Middle East. They continued to keep in touch after I left Aurora, and I still consider Ruth Dietrich my American mother.

At Aurora, as at Swansea, I found many excellent teachers who significantly contributed to my life. One was Dr. Stanley Perry, a magnificent scholar who knew how to instruct his students. His ancient history class began at 7:30 A.M. and he demanded that everyone be on time! Whenever someone was late he looked at his watch and said: "Good morning young man (lady). What is your excuse for being late?" Once he was not there when I arrived, so as a joke I sat down in his place. When others came, I mimicked his lines. When Dr. Perry entered, I looked at my watch and said: "Good morning young man. What is your excuse for being late?" Everyone laughed, but Dr. Perry had the last laugh. He told me to stay in his place and lecture. I said, "If I had known that, I wouldn't have done it to you." He would not relent, so I taught the class about the Middle East.

As students we enjoyed close, friendly relationships with our professors. During one of our class's social times, Dr. Perry had me cook Arabic food. Everyone enjoyed it, especially me. We have an Arabic saying: "There is between us bread and salt." Sharing meals brings people together. It spawns solidarity and affinity.

The good, friendly relationships with humble, caring faculty molded my personality. My majors, history and sociology, fascinated me and made me aware of the world and my niche. One semester, as a trainee, I taught high school United States history—a splendid opportunity for someone from the Middle East!

On one occasion Dr. James Crimi, Aurora's president, invited me to speak to the local Kiwanis Club. I enjoyed telling about my homeland and personal experiences until one man in the audience said I did not know what I was talking about. Many apologized for his discourtesy and expressed appreciation for presenting the side of the story they rarely heard. The experience reminded me that, as at Swansea, many people lack awareness of what Zionism did to the Palestinians.

In retrospect, 1960–63 were ideal years for me to have been in the United States. For three hundred years black Americans suffered at the hands of white Americans, much like Palestinians anguished under the Ottoman, British, and Israeli yokes. Yet during the early sixties in the United States, concerned people were beginning to act. Of the many leaders, no one stood out like the Rev. Martin Luther King, Jr.

I admired him. He openly faced the issues, and through the moral fervor of his message and the eloquence of its presentation, he led his people toward freedom. He grounded his Christlike teaching in biblical truths. I respected his courageous "direct action." I also appreciated the integrity of his call to loving nonviolence, even in the face of intimidation and violence. A few quotations from his book of sermons, *Strength to Love,* make a profound point:

Returning hate for hate multiplies hate, adding deeper darkness to a night already devoid of stars. Darkness cannot drive out darkness; only light can do that. Hate cannot drive out hate; only love can do that. Hate multiplies hate, violence multiplies violence, and toughness multiplies toughness in a descending spiral of destruction. So when Jesus says "Love your enemies," he is setting forth a profound and ultimately inescapable admonition. Have we not come to such an impasse in the modern world that we must love our enemies—or else? The chain reaction of evil—hate begetting hate, wars producing more wars—must be broken, or we shall be plunged into the dark abyss of annihilation.

Another reason why we must love our enemies is that hate scars the soul and distorts the personality. . . . Hate is just as injurious to the person who hates. . . . Hate destroys a man's sense of values and his objectivity. It causes him to describe the beautiful as ugly and the ugly as beautiful, and to confuse the true with the false and the false with the true. . . .

Love is the only force capable of transforming an enemy into a friend. We never get rid of an enemy by meeting hate with hate; we get rid of an enemy by getting rid of enmity. By its very nature, hate destroys and tears down; by its very nature love creates and builds up. Love transforms with redemptive power. . . .

We must hasten to say that these are not the ultimate reasons why we should love our enemies. . . . We must love our enemies, because only by loving them can we know God and experience the beauty of his holiness.[1]

Reading Martin Luther King, Jr.'s words deepened my conviction to work for the Palestinian people, but only with the love of Jesus in my heart. I felt called to help the helpless. I assessed my life's priorities with penetrating clarity: Jesus is Lord. I must do nothing without his blessing. Whatever my life's work, it must follow his leading. "Lord, I am willing to go anywhere in the world, and do whatever you want of me."

Yet, God did not direct me immediately to Palestine. Early in 1963 I read that seventeen missionary families of the United Presbyterian Church had been among three hundred evicted by the military dictatorship of the Sudan in East Africa. Suddenly I understood: I should go to the Sudan. I prayed, "Lord, you know where I stand," thanked him for his leading, and applied to the United Presbyterian Church's Commission on Ecumenical Mission and Relations in New York City. After many tests, including a long psychological examination, a physical, and an interview, I spent five intensive weeks at a missionary orientation center. They invited me to apply for a teaching position at the Sudan mission school and soon approved my application.

I still remember my last Sunday evening in June of 1963 at the First Presbyterian Church in Aurora, where I was served as pastoral assistant under Calvin Marcum, Robert Grupp's successor. These dear people, who had given me money for college three years earlier, held a beautiful dedication service. Their love and concern touched me deeply.

I vacationed in Ramallah before going to the Sudan during the summer of 1963. While there, I enjoyed reflecting, visiting, and fellowshipping. After four weeks I received instructions that I was to fly to Khartoum the following Monday.

As I sat around talking and saying good-bye to my friends that Sunday afternoon, I experienced a most pleasant shock. There, coming up the pathway, was Patricia Greening, my friend from Swansea. Emotion overwhelmed me when I saw her after five years. On furlough from missionary nursing in Peru, Patricia, with her parents, was visiting the Holy Land for a few days. I delighted in talking with this friend whose face I had often seen in my imagination, and to whom I had written at Christmas and birthdays. Patricia's warm personality, insights and commitment to God captivated me.

Suddenly, I had that familiar feeling—when God is saying something, telling me to trust him fully and he will work out the details. Before Patricia left that evening, I told her: "For five years I have been praying that God would lead me to the person he wants to be my wife. Always, before any others, I see your face, but I have thought it couldn't be, because we were so far from each other. But as I saw your face today, I knew! God seemed to say to me: 'There she is!'"

My sudden proposal shocked Patricia, but I knew that down deep she had always felt attracted to me. Marriage seemed out of the question, since God had called her to Peru and me to the Sudan (and perhaps eventually home to

Palestine), but I felt the same assurance as at other times when I have stepped out on faith. We briefly discussed marriage, then decided to write regularly, and determine God's will as time went by.

Even though her answer was only a "maybe," I left for the Sudan the next morning full of hope and anticipation. If God can provide a stamp, a bus ticket, or a college education, he can work out the details of bringing two people together. He had made a zillion light-years universe—the eight thousand miles between Peru and the Sudan should be a minor problem.

The American Mission High School was in Omdurman, near the mission headquarters in Khartoum in the northern part of the Sudan. In addition to the school, the mission compound housed the executive missionaries, a public library, and a church. I taught English, ancient history, modern history, church history, and the Arabic language—a very busy, enjoyable life of working with young people.

The difficult years in Africa taught me political science firsthand. The Sudan's cosmopolitan Moslem North contrasts with the primitive, isolated South. The Sudan is a diverse region. For over a half-century the British (the stronger member of an uneven alliance with Egypt) maintained a dominating political and military presence. Northern native elites, prosperous because of the British presence, were local functionaries in their rule. The British encouraged European Christian missionary activity, but barred indigenous Sudanese missionaries, traders, and teachers from the south.

A revolution in 1956 terminated Anglo-Egyptian control. After an unsuccessful attempt at republican government, a coup led by General Ibrahim Abbud in 1958 brought an authoritarian, home-based rule friendly to Egypt. Abbud's northern-based administration hoped to impose nationwide unity under Moslem law and culture, but faced opposition from most southerners and northern Christians, and from those who favored secular government. The new regime banned political parties and shifted education from English to Arabic and from Christian to Moslem.

In 1962 the government expelled many Christian missionaries, including the Presbyterians I had read about. Strikes and anti-government demonstrations broke out in southern schools the same year. General Abbud increased the repression. By 1963 the ugly southern mood intensified as violent rebellions occurred and met even harsher repression.

Meanwhile, northern intellectuals—some of whom had become communists—agitated for a more democratic government and a better life for the oppressed. In October of 1964 (one year after I arrived in the Sudan) students at the University of Khartoum launched major demonstrations against the government. The disorder intensified, forcing General Abbud to resign. For several weeks, various factions vied for control. By late 1964 the tides of revolution overflowed banks that could turn blood red.

Sunday afternoon, December 6, 1964, loudspeaker trucks announced an event of interest to southerners. The newly appointed Minister of Interior, a southerner, would appear at the airport at 3:30 P.M. Thousands went to hear what he would say. However, he did not arrive on schedule; after an hour passed, then another, the crowd became uneasy, then frightened. They feared their enemies had assembled them for a massacre. Skirmishes began at the airport, then outbreaks of violence spread throughout the city.

In the meantime, across town at a soccer match, the fans—fanatics—were becoming excited, drunk without drink. Near the end of the match a rumor, spread by factions that wanted to take over the government, circulated among the crowd.

Southerners were molesting wives and daughters of the soccer fans. This intensified the storm of violence, which had spread all over the area.

Meanwhile, we held a baptismal for forty southern converts in the mission compound. Gradually, we became aware of an angry mob—about twelve thousand people we later learned—forming outside the compound, wanting to attack the converts and members of their families. Then someone threw gasoline-filled glass bottles with ignited wicks. The library was on fire! We gathered the southerners and some missionaries inside an apartment for an intensive prayer meeting. We could not telephone outside—someone had cut the wires—and we could not leave because of the angry crowds. Yet, praying there together, we felt a sense of inner peace. Although isolated from human beings who could protect us, God was with us. Perhaps we might lose our lives, but we knew God's power was available as he chose to use it. The fire did not reach us, nor did the mob.

Late that night we decided to go home, thinking that the crowd had dispersed. However, when we opened the gate, the mob surrounded us, brandishing chains, knives, and clubs! We quickly jumped into the truck the Ministry of Interior had provided and escaped with minor injuries. Some of us went back the next morning and found everything black, with many buildings collapsed. When we left again, we met an angry mob at the gate; they grabbed and beat several of us with clubs, but everyone escaped. It certainly was a harrowing experience!

The ruin of the mission headquarters redirected my life. More and more my mind focused on the plight of my own people. As I prayed, God seemed to be telling me to return to Palestine, my homeland. Palestine had never been absent from my mind; this seemed the time to rejoin my people.

The memories of that experience in the Sudan have benefited me in recent years. The political situation was confusing; however, the core issue was a military tyranny under siege from discontented subjects. I have learned that people under oppression search until they find a solution. That lesson has had growing importance since the 1967 military occupation of the West Bank.

I returned to Ramallah after eighteen months' service in the Sudan. While there I visited the girls' home that missionaries from Swansea and the United States had established in 1954. When those missionaries—Keturah Morgan, Gladys Thomas, and Mary Jeanne Grupp—asked if I would leave Ramallah soon, I announced: "No. I am going to stay here and open a boys' home." "Praise the Lord," they responded, "Two weeks ago we took in a needy girl who has a twin brother named Tony. We haven't known what to do because we cannot care for boys. So your home already has its first boy!"

The Lord had spoken. A new chapter in my life was opening. It promised to be a delightful chapter, because Patricia had written with her decision: an enthusiastic *Yes!*

Left: Audeh as a student at Swansea in 1956
Right: Patricia Greening in Peru with Megan Jones, who saved many lives with delicate operations

Pat's father, Rev. Royden Greening, handing the couple their marriage certificate. With them are bridesmaid Margaret Wiles and best man John Cook. All four young people graduated from the Bible College of Wales and went to mission fields.

Audeh's father with Susan, 1968

A 1975 gathering of the entire Rantisi family males. Audeh is in the center of the front row. His father is seated in the front row, extreme left.

Audeh, Susan, Pat, Hilary, and Audeh's mother

Susan, Patricia, Audeh, and Hilary Rantisi

Patricia and Audeh

Patricia's parents on the occasion of Rev. Greening's eightieth birthday, 1983

Hilary with Omar, who grew up in a refugee
camp but spends lots of time with the Rantisis

Pat and Audeh with their first twelve boys. *Front row, left-to-right:*
Raymond, Sammie, Tony, Jamal, Khadir, Easa; *second row:* John, Elias,
Basil, Nasri, Jack, Peter

With former Arab Evangelical Episcopal Church Bishop Faik Haddad, breaking ground for the new building, 1978. Hilary is the child on the right.

Students from Teen Missions, Miami Springs, Florida, working on the new building in 1979

"هذا البناء، مكرس لمجد الله
إن لم يبنِ الرب البيت فباطلاً يتعب البناؤون"
ديسمبر ١٩٨٢

Except the LORD build the house,
they labour in vain that build it.
PSALM 127 v.1.

This building is dedicated to the
GLORY of GOD   DECEMBER 1982

The purpose of the Evangelical Home for Boys

Audeh and Vivian's son Elia, outside the new home

The Evangelical Home workers and children outside the house they
occupied from 1970 to 1988

The Evangelical Home for Boys in 1989

Some of the boys in the home

Boys singing around the piano with Daniel Burton, a house-father from England. *Left-to-right:* Remon, George, Elias, Hanna, Paul, and Salam

Lunch time at the Evangelical Home for Boys

Vivian, the home's cook, her son Elia, and other boys doing dishes

A delegation from Aurora University presented Audeh its 1977 "Alumnus of the Year" award. *Left-to-right:* Audeh, Orin Singleterry, Jeanette Cilkey, Ramallah Mayor Karim Khalaf, Farid Tawasha, Jad Mikhail.

Coauthors Audeh G. Rantisi and Ralph K. Beebe

Audeh and Ralph taping an interview

The Rantisis with Wanda and Ralph Beebe

The Hicks family, Glada, Todd, and Majida in Ramallah, February 25, 1990.

Invitation to a service of Thanksgiving and Dedication at the Home for Boys, April 23, 1990.

chapter five

Patricia

*A*T AGE twenty-eight my life came together. All my previous experiences and education seemed directed toward 1965, when I married and began my lifelong calling.

A child of eleven, lonely, bewildered, in need of a home; a boy of fourteen, eagerly accepting the opportunity to learn; a lad of fifteen, profoundly changed by the reality of Jesus Christ; a young man of eighteen, adventuring abroad in search of an education—these milestones measured my growth. Through the years I often pondered the lives of similar boys still in Ramallah. I always knew that God might lead me back someday.

In God's timing, events moved with astounding speed: the wild scene in Khartoum at the end of 1964, the decision to move to Palestine, the cooperation of the women at the Evangelical Home for Girls, and the letter from Patricia, revealing her love and desire to be my partner. The pathway lay before me by early 1965. I merely had to walk it.

Since then my life has been not one, but two: Patricia and Audeh. We share every dream, every hope, every accomplishment, every failure. We live as a team.

Born the daughter of an Anglican clergyman in England, Pat attended school there, eventually becoming a registered nurse. She tells about her spiritual experience in her own words:

When I was nineteen and in nursing school I had a close friend named Pat Tuffrey. We were separated during part of our training. When I saw her again I immediately saw that she had changed. I asked: "Pat, what has happened?" She responded: "Oh, I've got a lot to tell you. Something has happened."

Then she revealed that God had come into her life—she had accepted Jesus as her Saviour. Earlier, she had been a very worldly girl, with no interest in Christianity. Then she met some Christians who impressed her greatly. She began to read the Bible, went to evangelistic meetings, and soon met Jesus.

This was a big shock! Here I was, brought up in a Christian home, but never actually having accepted Jesus personally. So that night she prayed for me and I opened the door to Christ. He came into my life as I committed myself fully to him. I experienced a major turning point. Following that, I became very active in Christian fellowship and started going out and giving my testimony. I was a very shy, timid person and could hardly face an audience.

The first time I gave my testimony was in an open-air meeting on a cloudy, threatening day. No one came to hear us, so I spoke only to the group of Christians and to the trees. Still, it was a start. After that I felt called to be a missionary, so I decided to go to the Bible college at Swansea.

After graduating, Patricia spent five years in Peru with Regions Beyond mission. As a nurse in a small mission hospital, she had marvelous opportunities to help needy people. Her coworker, a nurse named Megan Jones, had trained herself as a surgeon, performing many operations because no medical doctor was available. For her part, Patricia worked with Peruvians at the hospital and in their homes, ministering to their spiritual and physical needs, and delivering hundreds of babies:

> We would work all week in the hospital, sometimes delivering babies all night. Then on weekends we went on horse or muleback three or four hours (probably 40–50 miles) into the jungle where we did medical work and preaching. The people

lived in primitive conditions, with little mud huts and no furniture. At first I had a blow-up air mattress, but eventually I felt more comfortable sleeping on the floor like the rest of the people.

During this time I occasionally wrote to Patricia, but I had not seen her since we left Swansea and went our separate ways. Then came that God-directed meeting in Ramallah. Pat describes it from her perspective:

In 1963 I was on furlough, at home in England. Unexpectedly, my father received a gift from a parishioner—a trip to the Holy Land—enough money to include my mother and me. At first I thought I wouldn't go, but after prayer I thought I should. Perhaps God had a purpose for me beyond just seeing the holy places.

Through the years Audeh had written occasionally, always remembering me on my birthday and at Christmas. Still, although I liked and appreciated him very much, I was not aware that he was the reason God directed me on this trip. While in Jerusalem, I made it a point to arrange a visit with Gladys Thomas and Kit Morgan, two friends from Swansea who were running a girls' home in Ramallah. While visiting them I asked: "By the way, do you know if Audeh Rantisi is in town?" My hostess replied: "Well, you know what, he is off to the Sudan tomorrow, but he is here today." So she took me to his house. I will always remember the shocked look—and the pleasure—on Audeh's face when he first saw me.

We talked all afternoon. Then, near the time for me to leave, Audeh told me of his prayers that God would lead him to the right girl. Always, he said, my face appeared before any others. "When I saw you coming today, God seemed to say: 'There she is!'" So, we had only that one afternoon together. The next time I saw him was almost two years later, when he came to England for our wedding.

I assure you that I was a very confused young lady that night—and for weeks to come! I just couldn't imagine that this could really be the Lord's will. He had called me to Peru. Yet as the months went by, I began to see his directing hand.

When I returned to Peru in 1964, a variety of circumstances had made the situation very different and no longer the fulfillment of my calling. Eventually, I became aware that God's voice was speaking to me, reinforcing my love for Audeh, impressing his homeland on my consciousness, tenderly calling me to work with him. So, in full assurance of God's will, I wrote to Audeh that I would love to be his wife and to spend my life sharing his vision and his ministry.

Pat's letter excited me more than any I had ever received. We set May 1, 1965, for our wedding. A month before that I journeyed to England to see her for only the second time since 1958.

We celebrated our marriage in the Meole Brace Parish Church in Shrewsbury, where her father, the Rev. Royden Greening, was minister. He conducted our service, reading from Psalm 121: "I will lift up mine eyes to the hills from whence cometh my help. My help cometh from the Lord." I thought of Ramallah, "the hill of God," where King David undoubtedly walked, pondering his psalms three thousand years ago. Maybe he wrote that one in Ramallah. "The Lord shall preserve thy going out, and thy coming in from this time forth forevermore," David said. Make it so, Lord; make our going out and coming in glorify thee.

The minister and congregation blessed us:

O Lord, save Thy servant and Thy handmaid, who put their trust in thee; O Lord, send them help from Thy holy place, and evermore defend them. Be unto them a tower of strength from the face of their enemy. O Lord, hear our prayer and let our cry come unto Thee.

As the service closed the congregation sang our commitment to God's will in our marriage and throughout our lives:

O Jesus I have promised to serve thee to the end. . . .

O let me hear thee speaking in accents clear and still, above the storms of passion, the murmurs of self-will; O speak to reassure me, to hasten or control; O speak, and make me listen, Thou guardian of my soul.

I embarked upon my life's calling secure in God's love and leading, knowing that he joined me in choosing Patricia. After a honeymoon in North Wales, we took a ship for the Gulf of Aqaba. There we were driven north to Amman, and crossed the Jordan River to our homeland.

Pat's father died in 1984, but her mother still lives, and we enjoy seeing her whenever we can. I appreciate her reactions to her daughter's choice of a husband:

> I didn't have trouble accepting Audeh, because I already knew him from Bible school and appreciated him a lot. However, when it first became known that Patricia was going to marry an Arab, some people reacted very negatively. There is a lot of prejudice in England.
>
> Also, the marriage worried some of our friends, who feared having her go to a culture so different from her own. I reminded them that she had lived in the Peruvian jungle for several years. Also, she at least knew something about the special problems of the Middle East, although I am sure she didn't fully realize all the ramifications of marrying into a different culture. But her father and I felt quite comfortable.
>
> I am very appreciative of Dr. Ieuan Jones, a Bible teacher whom Patricia respected immensely. He spoke briefly at the wedding, telling of his high regard for both Audeh and Patricia. He assured everyone this was truly a Christian marriage, one that would have good unity in spite of the cultural differences. I cherish what this fine man said, and how in the presence of our friends, it reinforced the rightness of the marriage. His assurances have certainly proved accurate.

The work in the new boys' home was difficult but rewarding. The Home of the Sons, where I lived from 1951 to 1955 and worked from 1958 to 1960, provided a model.

However, the girls' home that Keturah Morgan, Gladys Thomas, and Mary Jeanne Grupp established in 1954 became the real parent (or sister) of our work. Along with women from Britain, Switzerland, Holland, Germany, France, the United States, and Palestine, these three ladies successfully attempted to meet the spiritual, educational, and physical needs of refugee Palestinian children. They temporarily closed the girls' home during the war following the invasion of the Suez Canal in 1956. However, the next year it reopened, affiliated with the Arab Evangelical Episcopal Church.

Early in 1965 the women managing the girls' home announced our plans in their newsletter:

> Audeh Rantisi, whom many of you know, is a Jordanian [the West Bank was then under Jordan], thus an answer to our prayer of years for a dedicated national coworker. Audeh was brought up in a home for boys, and trained in the Bible College of Wales, so he has learned in a very practical way the life of faith. He has a degree in sociology and education from the States, and has had the experience of serving as a house-master, and teaching in the Sudan another two years.
>
> May 1, Audeh married Patricia Greening of Shrewsbury. Patricia, also known to many of you, is an S.R.N., has been trained in the Bible College of Wales, and afterward served as a missionary in Peru. Audeh and Patricia feel called to take the responsibility for our new Home for Boys. We know that you will rejoice over God's gracious leading and provision for the needy boys of Jordan. Please pray for wisdom and guidance that all will be in accord with God's perfect pattern for this work.

Patricia and I appreciated the support of these fine women who heroically ran both the home for girls and an associated evangelical Christian school. Our rewarding and mutually beneficial relationship continues.

We felt that our ministry—the Evangelical Home for Boys—got off to a good start. Seeing God's will in the work, we felt content. Yet we constantly wished we could help more young people. Perhaps my memories of 1948 made this even more poignant. I always wanted to help solve the enormous problems faced by Palestinians still suffering from the political disruptions.

Patricia's commitment and concern for human beings inspired me. She faced many adjustments as we moved into our new home with twelve instant "sons," but she displayed an exceptional ability to adapt to unusual and difficult circumstances.

From the beginning we disdained appeals for funds to support our home for boys. If God directed our work, we should not beg. He would meet our needs. However, we did send an occasional newsletter telling friends of our progress. Patricia wrote the first in October of 1965. It provided an interesting history of our early experiences and our reactions to them:

> The house is a semi-bungalow type with five main rooms and one attic room upstairs. It is in a very central spot of the town and stands on its own with spacious grounds for the children to play in.
>
> We had just a month to prepare for the children, and were glad to have that time for there was much to do in getting the house ready to make it a home. Our family of twelve boys arrived on September 1st, and never shall we forget those first few difficult days, but somehow the Lord undertook for us and now we can truly say that the boys have settled down well and seem very happy together. Now that we have got to know each child individually, we have grown to love them, and our one desire is to see them grow up to know the Lord Jesus as their Saviour. We have one helper, a young woman whom we employed originally just to cook for us all, but who has

become a willing helper with the washing and other domestic chores. She is non-resident.

Let me tell you a little about our boys, so that you can pray for them. Our youngest is Tony, only three, who was first admitted to the Girls' Home and was already waiting for us. He comes from a broken home and is a difficult child to understand. He is the only one who does not go to school, for they start at the kindergarten branch of our Evangelical School when four years old. Then there is Sammie, aged four, a very lovable, sunny child, but full of mischief! Sammie's mother died soon after his birth. Jamal, aged five, is no trouble and a sweet little boy; but Easa, also five, is very nervous, a child needing much love and trust. Khadir (St. George), almost six, is mentally backward but eats like a horse! Basil, only five, is a big boy for his age and acts older too. Next comes Jack, six, a nice boy, though strongwilled. His father is dead. Raymond's father, now dead, was an Italian. Raymond, six and one-half, is very small for his age, but looks up to one with a round rosy face and big shining eyes, full of intelligence. He is doing very well at school. Hanna (John), seven, is quiet but not very bright, and needs much encouragement and help. Peter and Elias are the same age, eight years old, but Peter is a very big boy and tries to be the big boss of the family, whereas Elias is quiet and slow. That leaves Nasri, nine, a very sensible, nice, intelligent boy who will go far.

Please pray for our family of boys, and for us too of course. We feel it is a wonderful privilege to bring up little ones in a Christian home, but it is also a tremendous responsibility. Pray for me (Patricia), as I endeavor to learn the Arabic language, and for Audeh as he has opportunity of teaching Scripture to four classes of boys and girls in a nearby high school.

Patricia suffered through much hardship, more than she revealed to me at the time. Her recent thoughts about those early months display determination and flexibility:

Our first year of marriage required much adjustment. I knew Audeh was Middle Eastern and that we were different, but I didn't really understand that people here expect the man to be so dominant. The English family is more equal. At first I encountered difficulties, to put it mildly. I had to adjust my way of thinking. His role was to lay down the law and mine was to follow without arguments.

I didn't know the culture. As soon as we had our first home, we already had twelve little boys—fourteen of us in a three-bedroom house. In Peru, I had been my own master and gave orders to the nurses and other people. This situation was totally different.

Patricia longed for a child of her own but did not become pregnant quickly. The meddlesome remarks of relatives, friends, and even strangers exacerbated the frustration of childlessness. Every time she served a cup of coffee to visitors, they would say *Andik walad*—"May you have a son!" This was their way of saying thank you for the coffee, but the daily reminder angered her. This is how she remembers it:

In this society they expect that you will have a baby immediately. Well, it didn't happen that way with me. His relatives kept coming to our house and asking me why I wasn't pregnant yet. In English society, this is something very private. You don't talk about it. You don't go and ask people why they haven't had a baby yet! Here, they do. It annoyed me and made me cross, to say the least. Why should they intrude on our private affairs? I even asked Naimeh Rizgallah, the lady who cooked for us, because I really didn't comprehend it at all. But now I understand the culture. It wasn't that they were intruding, it was just that they were concerned for us. Now I understand and appreciate their way of thinking.

I felt very much alone sometimes. I spoke no Arabic and none of our twelve boys spoke any English. Nor did Naimeh, with whom I spent several hours every day, helping to cook food I hadn't as yet learned to like. However, I did have fellowship and prayer meetings, in English, with some of the women from the Girls' Home. Audeh conversed with me in English. Meanwhile, I gradually learned the Arabic language and customs. I had some tutoring, but mostly I just picked up the language on my own. I wish now that I had taken the proper course from the school, but my twelve boys kept me too busy.

Pat marvelously adjusted to the new culture and our houseful of dependents. Gradually becoming aware of her frustration, I also grew and learned to help her adjust. Through the years we both learned to compromise and help each other face difficult experiences.

My relatives' eagerness and overprotectiveness bewildered Patricia and seemed meddlesome and intrusive from the English perspective. Yet, in encouraging us to have children, they were looking out for her and for me. Family is immensely important in the Middle Eastern culture—far more so than in Western Europe or the United States.

Our culture centers on the family—so much so that the oldest son of an oldest son is named after the grandfather. Thus, the oldest grandson carries his grandfather's name. My grandfather's name is Audeh, and had I a son, his oldest son would also be named Audeh. So, from the cultural stand-point, failure to have a boy reflected on Patricia. Over the years we had three daughters—Susan, Hilary, and Rose-mary—but never a son. However, whenever anyone seemed concerned, we joked: "But we have a whole houseful of sons!"

Our first two years of marriage were hardly a honeymoon. I am sure we experienced more stress than most newlyweds. But we may have had more joy, because ours was a joyous calling.

Yet we could not predict the severe wrenching that began in June of 1967. Once again, Palestinians faced a disaster from which we still have not recovered.

chapter six

War!

*T*O US as well as to the rest of the Middle East, the year 1967 brought tension and tears. We were again the victims of a war.

Ramallah, unconquered by Israel in 1948–49, is in the part of Palestine called the West Bank. It became a possession of Jordan. Both the British mandate and the United Nations' partition plan promised a national homeland for the Palestinians, but it never happened.

Since 1949 the Palestinians and the Jordanians who ruled us had experienced continual friction. Israel and all the neighboring Arab nations also were subject to constant tension. By the spring of 1967 the future looked ominous. Then, in June, bursting on us with lightning speed came the Six-Day War.

War is a nightmare. As a child I experienced years of dreadful dreams about 1948. I suppose the children of 1967 also have night terrors. We all live daily with the tragic results. Israeli occupation of the West Bank and Gaza Strip since 1967 has reaped a bitter harvest of ill-will and resentment. The uprising that began late in 1987—the intifada— predictably resulted.

The causes of the 1967 war are not difficult to trace. Tension had been growing in the Arab world since the beginning of Zionism. Massive Jewish immigration since

World War I, the United Nations' partition plan after World War II, and the 1948 war between the Arab nations and Israel severely shattered Palestinian security, creating an awful dread of further Zionist expansion. Arabs feared that the Israelis would soon attempt to fulfill the Zionist interpretation of God's promise to Abraham: that eventually only his Jewish descendants would occupy all the land from the Nile in Egypt to the Euphrates in Iraq.

The 1967 war followed the one in 1956, when Israel created a pretext for attacking Egypt. Defense Minister Moshe Dayan later admitted that Israel intended to find "any politically favorable opportunity to strike at Egypt."[1] Only strong diplomatic action and threats by United States President Eisenhower forced Israel to give up lands it had taken in the Sinai.

However, for Israel, 1956 was a rehearsal for a more decisive war eleven years later. By then the Zionist nation was nineteen years old, and an entire generation had grown up with a paranoid, militaristic mentality. If security was threatened, they were ready to strike first and ask questions later— and in the Israeli mindset, security is always being threatened, no matter how small the provocation. Centuries of victimization and discrimination have made paranoia a way of life for Jews. (However, the Arab mind always carries a countervailing fear of Zionist expansionism, similar to the Western world's fear of communism.)

By 1967 many leaders in Israel, fearful of the Arab states and anxious for recognition as a major power, relished the chance for war. Nationalism also ran high in Nasser's Egypt and other Middle Eastern countries. The Arab nations bristled, anxious to counter a whole century of European imperialism and a generation of Israeli threats. Through the spring, epithets flew in each direction.

The most significant provocation came on May 23, 1967. Egyptian President Nasser decided to reimpose an earlier blockade on the Straits of Tiran, part of Egypt's territorial waters in the Gulf of Aqaba. The Gulf closing, although the embarkation point of only five percent of Israel's shipping, did jeopardize her ambition to increase trade with Africa and Asia. More important, it threatened the Israeli psyche, which found backing down before any Arab state unthinkable—especially in view of Israel's much better armaments.

Early in the morning of June 5, 1967, Israel launched an aerial blitzkrieg, a first strike that destroyed 400 Egyptian jets on the ground and all but won the war in four hours. The Israeli army and air force, massively equipped with American military supplies, outgunned the Arab nations and in six days occupied the Gaza Strip, the Golan Heights, Jerusalem, and the West Bank (including Ramallah). The 57 percent of Palestine originally given to the Zionists had grown to 77 percent in the 1948–49 war. Now the Israelis took military control of the other 23 percent.

Patricia and I had celebrated our second wedding anniversary the preceding May 1, and completed our second school year with our boys. As is the case each summer, most of the boys went to live temporarily with their extended families—a policy that discourages dependency and provides a sense of family.

Pat anticipated a summer vacation in England, where she could enjoy a good visit with her parents. We had already purchased tickets when war became imminent. Therefore, we decided that she should try to leave a few days early. Then we learned of a Christian tour bus that authorities ordered to leave after only one day in the Holy Land. We quickly arranged space for Pat and another lady from the girls' school.

Patricia gave her distant view of the 1967 war in an

interesting newsletter from Shrewsbury, England, on June 19:

> "Pray for the peace of Jerusalem, they shall prosper that love thee."
>
> It is with a very burdened heart for the people of Jordan that I write you this letter from England.
>
> The lightning war in the Middle East has left us all very bewildered and we do not know what the future of our work will be.
>
> However, although we feel deeply for the thousands of sorrowing hearts in Jerusalem, we still have much to Praise the Lord for in his protection of us. Only five days before the fighting began, the Lord opened up a rather unexpected, but wonderful way of coming to England. . . . As we hurriedly left Jerusalem early Wednesday morning, May 31, we saw lorry loads of young men being taken into the army and then we were caught up in a convoy of tanks heading for the frontiers. We passed through seven countries—Syria, Turkey, Bulgaria, Yugoslavia, Germany and Belgium, finally crossing the Channel to England.
>
> On our arrival in London on Friday 9th June, the war was virtually over. It was not until three days later that I learned that my husband, Audeh, was safe, our Home intact. However, tragic news was to follow: I heard that four of my colleagues from the Girls' Home had been flown home, injured during a bombing raid; two of the girls, aged twelve and eighteen, had been killed, and the main building of the Girls' Home was demolished. We do not yet know if all our children are safe, because they are scattered in different towns with their relatives, and some of them are now isolated on the East Bank of Jordan. Ramallah, as you have probably realized, is on the West Bank, which is the part occupied, at present, by the Israelis.
>
> School is due to re-open in August, but of course, everything now depends on what happens politically in the Middle East. No doubt there will be more needy families than ever before, and one's desire is to help them and continue our

witness. We believe that God is even now using our children as a testimony. Little Raymond, age eight, when his mother asked why he had broken up from school a week earlier, replied "Because there is no peace in this world, Mummy." He reads the Bible to his brothers and sisters every day.

Please continue to pray that the door of witness may remain open in the Holy Land and that our work will go forward.

P.S. Miss Mary-Jeanne Grupp and Miss Doris Leafe are now receiving treatment in a hospital in Swansea.

During the nine-day trip Patricia heard some disturbing news about the war, but had no specific word from home. Then, she looked out the window as the bus stopped at the square in Salzburg, Austria, on June 6. Amazingly, just outside was Robert Grupp, our dear friend who directed The Home of the Sons where I had lived fifteen years earlier. What a shock! Neither knew the other was within a thousand miles of Salzburg. Surprised, they exchanged greetings, and he told her radio reports said that Ramallah had been under fire and taken by the Israelis that day. He did not know at the time that the Girls' Home had been shelled, killing the two girls mentioned in our newsletter, and wounding his sister and several others.

Soon after Patricia arrived in England, the Shrewsbury newspaper featured us in a front page lead article. Headlined "Shellfire Hits Jordan School," the article carried our picture and began:

> Three days after the daughter of the vicar of Meole Brace arrived back in Shrewsbury, she heard that the school which she and her husband run in Ramallah in Jordan had been hit by gunfire.
>
> Two girls at the school were killed and four seriously wounded companions were flown to this country. . . .
>
> Information at the moment is very sketchy.

Meanwhile, in Ramallah I experienced my second dreadful

war. Nineteen years had not erased the horror of our eviction and forced march. The ominous feeling returned as alien soldiers again invaded my home village in June 1967. Would our children have to experience my bitter childhood fate? Thankfully, most were away from Ramallah for the summer, living with extended families. Still, wherever they were, danger undoubtedly threatened. I prayed and tried to trust, but felt uneasy.

That Tuesday, June 6, my younger brother, Mahfouz, and I were working on our house when we heard the sound of a plane. He opened the door, but I called to him to close it—just in time, because a bomb exploded nearby. Later we joined other families in a one-story house with thick walls and remained there until the fighting ended. The shelling shattered the whole area. Many buildings, including the evangelical girls' home, suffered damage. Meanwhile, lacking any kind of tools, our pastor, the Rev. Eliya Khoury, dug graves with his hands for the two girls from our school.

With the West Bank under Israeli military control, Patricia could not return through Jordan. I telephoned her to come through Tel Aviv instead. However, a new law required Palestinians to have permits for going anywhere outside the West Bank, even for a day. I was prohibited from meeting Patricia's plane when she returned in early September, because Tel Aviv is in Israel. Thankfully, William Ross, an American who taught at the Friends Boys' School, offered his help. I decided to risk driving to the airport with him. We picked up Patricia without incident.

However, on the way home soldiers stopped us. In the confusion of a new occupation, the authorities were uncertain about what to do with West Bank Palestinians. They detained us for several hours, saying they would not allow us to return home. Finally they let us go, but it was too late to reach

Ramallah before the sundown curfew imposed by the new military government on all Palestinians.

Three army jeeps stopped us at the turning of the road that led to our home. Soldiers quickly surrounded our car, their guns pointed menacingly. I tried to explain our problem, but did not get much of a hearing. Eventually they directed us to the military governor whom Israel had placed in power. After some discussion, he let us go home.

I enjoyed having Patricia home, but the third year with our boys began under a cloud of military occupation. We could not predict what would happen. How well I remembered my father and grandfather nineteen years earlier: the initial anticipation of a quick return to Lydda, then the mounting frustration as one by one the empty months passed. Disappointment gradually turned to despair for them. In 1967 we again hoped for a quick settlement and withdrawal of Israeli military forces, but experience had taught skepticism.

Still, we knew we must endure, despite adverse circumstances. Our calling—to help young people—remained strong, and the need intensified. We were sure that God would continue to provide for our material, spiritual, and emotional needs.

Our mood—somber yet hopeful—permeated our newsletter of November 1967:

Dear Friends,

Once again, as the Christmas season approaches, we want to wish you all: A VERY HAPPY CHRISTMAS and a BLESSED NEW YEAR. . . .

We would like to thank you all for the sustaining influence of your prayers in these difficult days. After three months in England, Patricia returned to Ramallah, via Israel, at the end of August. Two weeks afterward, we were to receive the children back into the Home. However, out of our twelve boys, only five returned. This was because most of the others are on the East Bank of the Jordan, now isolated from us because of the division of the country after the Middle East War. We, in Ramallah, are on the West Bank, which is in the part at present occupied by the Israelis.

We are terribly sad not to have all our boys back and although we have taken in two new boys, making our number seven, we feel our Home is not the same without the others! Although we cannot contact them to know how they are, our prayers are daily with them.

The situation is, of course, still very unsettled, but we are happy to say that our school is continuing as before, in spite of a delay in opening. The new school building is now in the process of being built and should be ready for use by next September, God willing.

Perhaps, by the time you get this letter, there may be more hope of a peaceful settlement, but our conviction is that only His Peace can solve every problem. We are reminded again of that Christmas hymn:

> Peace on earth, and mercy mild,
> God and sinners reconciled . . .

May the Lord continue to bless and guide us all. Thank you again for all your loving thoughts, prayers and gifts.

Yours sincerely,
Audeh and Patricia Rantisi

P.S. Please note our address: via Israel.

So we faithfully continued our work, constantly hoping the army would leave. The United Nations Security Council agreed with us. It passed Resolution 242, which condemned Israel's military occupation and called for withdrawal. However, the resolution made no mention of a Palestinian state, and with that silence once again sold out the interests of my people.

Furthermore, the Israelis disregarded the United Nations' demands, choosing instead to create facts by establishing a major Jewish presence on the militarily occupied West Bank.

They gradually built about 135 subsidized apartment areas called settlements, each with space for up to 10,000 Jewish immigrants from throughout the world. Since 1967 at least 70,000 Jews have immigrated to the West Bank and another 2,500 to the Gaza Strip. In 1990 they made plans for many thousands of Soviet Jews to settle in the West Bank. The settlement policy is more than an attempt to meet a need for good housing for Jews. It aims for the Zionist movement to eventually control all Palestine, and to menace other Arab lands as well.

The war and the settlements devastated Palestinians. Though life had not been easy under the Ottomans, the British, and the Jordanians, the Israeli military occupation grieved us much more. My father and grandfather's dream of an independent Palestine—a homeland where Palestinians can live in freedom—remains unfulfilled.

Military Occupation

S HOCK waves hit us immediately. Israel made a law classifying all Palestinians who were outside the West Bank and Gaza Strip on June 5, 1967, as "absentees." No absentee can return home unless he or she has relatives there, and then only for a visit.

Two of my brothers were absent—Philip working in Kuwait, Elias in the United States—and now, although they were born in Palestine, they cannot live at home. This law especially affects Moslem Arabs with no immediate families in the occupied territories. It prohibits them from making the hajj, the pilgrimage to Jerusalem, one of Islam's holy shrines. This directly denies Moslems an important religious freedom.

Early Sunday morning, March 2, 1969, a member of our congregation telephoned, paraphrasing John 20:2: "They have taken the master away and we don't know where they have put him." (She used those words because the military government had our phone lines tapped.) I rushed to the church and learned that soldiers had come during the night and arrested Pastor Eliya Khoury for speaking out against the human rights violations. Because Pastor Khoury still had the church keys, I conducted an outdoor service that morning.

The occupation authorities also subjected Palestinians to an increasing number of military laws, which by 1990 numbered well over twelve hundred. Until the intifada they usually enforced those laws only as needed to maintain control; therefore, the casual visitor may not have noticed. We see the evidence clearly, however, because it is a conscious policy to make us feel inferior, to keep us a subjugated underclass, and to encourage us to leave.

For example: the Israeli military and many civilians arm themselves, but Palestinians face imprisonment for possession of a weapon; Israel guarantees basic human rights for Jews, but Arabs in the West Bank and Gaza Strip face arrest for protesting, or for failure to carry identification cards; Israelis have full property rights, while Palestinians live in fear that authorities will confiscate their farms, businesses, and homes; economic opportunities abound for Israelis, but the law prohibits Palestinians from owning businesses that compete with Jews; Israelis have a nation, but Palestinians have only a dream.

Another punitive factor is that water is at a premium in this arid country. Irrigation allotments for Israelis far exceed those of the Palestinians—and Israelis pay half our rate. The government provides Israelis with marketing subsidies that are unavailable to Palestinians. More than a hundred thousand West Bank and Gaza Strip residents commute as day laborers to Israel; their Jewish employers pay them about half the wages Israelis receive. (As a "security precaution," authorities prohibit West Bank and Gaza Strip Palestinians from staying overnight in Israel, forcing a difficult commute to work.) Many Palestinians pay twenty percent of their wages into the Israeli social security system, but receive no benefits. In fact, through taxes and social security payments West Bank and Gaza Strip residents subsidize Israel with about $80 million a year.[1]

Many regulations directly affect Palestinians; others do not.

Here is an example of one that does: Israeli cars have yellow license plates, West Bank Arabs blue, so that police can spot Palestinians. A number of times police stopped me for speeding but did not bother yellow licenses going as fast. It is hard to prove, but Palestinians believe that such actions are principally attempts to intimidate.

Of the many disabilities, one of the worst is the Zionists' strike at the property Palestinians have as families. A house is not just mortar and stone, four walls, and a roof to us. It symbolizes our inheritance, our identity, our culture, our dignity. Some Israelis try to uproot us in order to destroy that which makes us what we are. However, I doubt that most Israelis, with foreign backgrounds, understand the prime importance of land and the extended family in Middle Eastern culture.

Since 1967 the occupiers have confiscated large areas of land without remuneration and bulldozed thousands of houses. Then, on our own land, they built the massive fortress-apartments that now surround all of our cities. Although United Nations Security Council Resolutions 242 and 338 condemned occupation of the West Bank and Gaza Strip, the government was intent on establishing a permanent Israeli presence—one invulnerable to demands from the United Nations or anyone else.

In building these massive settlements that now claim over half the West Bank, they intend to restrict the Arab population by confining Palestinians to a ghetto-like environment. Through this they hope to encourage Palestinian emigration. Seeing themselves as modern-day Zionists and pioneers of Jewish expansionism, these defiant right-wing colonists express the most arrogant, intransigent, and bigoted attitudes of all Israelis. By successfully thumbing their noses at the United

Nations, they have created delusions of their own invincibili-
ty.

Foreign Minister Shamir asserted: "We want peace but
only in conditions that will enable us to continue our
existence, and this means the Golan Heights, Judea, and
Samaria [the West Bank] within the borders of the Land of
Israel."[2] In 1981 the government projected 120,000 to
150,000 settlers by 1986.[3] (They reached only about half the
goal.)

Fifteen years after the occupation began, Prime Minister
Menachem Begin scolded Knesset members who expressed
moral concerns:

> Settlement . . . almost one hundred years ago, in areas of the
> Land of Israel populated by Arabs and sometimes solely by
> Arabs—was it moral or immoral? Permitted or forbidden?
> One of the two. . . . If [it] was moral, and we all boast of one
> hundred years of settlement, then today's settlement near
> Nablus, Jericho, and Bethlehem [that is, the West Bank] is
> moral. Or do you have a double standard?[4]

Military authorities often apply a cruel technique called
"collective punishment." When they accuse someone of an
"illegal" act, they punish the entire family, or perhaps the
whole community. Sometimes they beat parents when children misbehave (by throwing rocks at Israeli cars, for
example). They hope to intimidate innocent people into
passivity, or even into retribution against fellow Palestinians.
They reason that frightened people will keep their children
and neighbors submissive to military authority. Conversely,
they reward collaborators.

Twice in 1976 the military placed Ramallah under curfew,
once for eleven days, again for thirteen. We often heard shots
as the army patrolled continuously, looking for suspected
subversives.

Tragedy missed by inches. We entertained more than fifty visitors at that time, and someone opened the kitchen door to let in cooler air. Unfortunately, several soldiers were patrolling the upper road in back. Immediately they shot into the kitchen. The bullet hit the cabinet less than six inches from one woman's head. The mark of that shell stayed in our kitchen cabinet as long as we lived there—a visible scar on our relationship with the Zionists.

Some days loudspeakers announced an hour's reprieve, so we could get relief from the indoor heat and go buy groceries. However, because we could never anticipate the brief respite, we could not prepare. One day at 9:00 A.M. they would broadcast from trucks that we could go outside for an hour. Immediately, all the people would run to the shops; if they lived at a distance, they might not get back on time and would be in trouble. The next day we would be ready at the same time, but nothing might happen, so we would wait until 10:00, then 11:00, and sometimes all afternoon. However, most days they would let us escape our dreary confinement for at least thirty minutes.

A curfew closed our Evangelical School for almost two weeks in May of 1976. The children could not go to school nor even play in the garden. About six o'clock in the morning one of our boys, Larry, went to the backyard with some garbage. A few moments later I saw him going toward the outside gate with his hands in the air, followed by five soldiers with guns pointed at him. When I asked why, the soldiers responded that the boy had broken the curfew. I told them this was an institution for needy children, and that we had done nothing wrong.

However, they insisted on taking him to the military police station. Horror-stricken, I argued some more. After searching me, they allowed me to accompany Larry. They would not let us talk; whenever I tried, they pressed their guns against me. Strangely, though, I felt secure in the Lord, and told the soldiers: "You don't frighten me with that piece of metal. If you are human beings, you will let us communicate." Still, however, they would not allow it.

At military headquarters one of the officers recognized me. He told the soldiers that I was a *Komer* (a gentile priest, or minister), so they took us home. I invited the soldiers to come in and have a cup of tea, but they said that they were on duty, and then left.

This incident is especially poignant to me because Larry was eleven, the same age I was when driven from my home. Having knowledge of what the authorities sometimes do to boys they consider subversive, I felt deep concern for Larry, and antagonism toward the soldiers.

Pat, also, had a harrowing experience during the 1976 curfew. She remembers:

> Doing the laundry was a real trial during curfews and our large family soon ran out of clean clothing. In normal times we washed inside, then hung the laundry on the roof. However, during curfew they made it illegal to go to the roof, so Audeh and I worked out a plan. I would take the clothes to the roof, and he would watch through the window and give a signal if any soldiers approached. Then I would run back into the house. One day, though, he didn't see the soldiers coming. I looked down and there they were, going into the house next door to get some food! I fell flat on my face, partially hidden by the wall around the roof. I waited for some time, sure they would shoot me if they caught me. Luckily they didn't.

After 1976 the military government discontinued major curfews. Apparently, the method had not achieved the anticipated results. They imposed only a few minor curfews after that, until the more extreme iron-fist policy that began in 1988 (when they curfewed some refugee camps for forty-eight days). Yet relief from curfews did not mean the military laws had changed. The soldiers enforced some regulations regularly, others sporadically.

The military governors mostly used the laws to intimidate the young people, whom they considered potential trouble-makers. They often closed universities for several days. Occasionally they shut down all West Bank and Gaza Strip schools, kindergarten through college. This was just a foretaste of the long school closures that began in 1988.

Patricia and I continued to care for our boys, recognizing God's call to obedience in spite of the circumstances. We revealed our mixed hope and frustration in our Christmas newsletter of 1973—the year of another Middle East war:

> We lament at this Christmas time that there is so little peace. Yet this land to which the Prince of Peace came as a baby, and where He lived and died for the world has never known peace. Throughout history it has been the greatest trouble spot on the earth, and once again we find ourselves in this state of war.
>
> As individuals, we can have peace in our hearts by acknowledging Jesus as Lord and Savior of our lives. Meanwhile we pray that peaceful settlement may be found very soon, and that people may be able to live together happily.

In considering our experiences during the first decade of occupation, my mind always returned to my calling: to serve God and my fellow human beings. What should be my contribution? The need is so immense. I have had such extraordinary opportunities. How can I serve most effectively? How can I help bring justice? How can I help prevent the seemingly inevitable bloodshed?

Pondering these questions I decided to become involved in politics as a candidate for city council in 1976. This decision brought discomfort, excitement, frustration, some danger, and an opportunity to witness the love of Jesus to Jews as well as Palestinians, to Moslems as well as Christians.

chapter eight

Politics

I ADMIT that I felt some uncertainty when in 1976 Mayor Karim Khalaf asked me to run for city council. I immediately explained that I did not want to seek office—my calling was to minister in my church and our home, which by then cared for thirty-six boys. He was insistent, however, so I told him that I needed to consult with someone. Two days later he asked again, pleading with me to run and wanting to know with whom I had consulted. I told him that I had consulted with the Lord.

I never had been comfortable doing less than I could; maybe this was God's leading, his opening into further service. Patricia and I prayed much and talked with our closest friends. Most Christians who influenced us were quite negative, thinking politics was divisive, an invitation to trouble—that I should concentrate on the gospel, not politics. This opinion was especially strong among the foreign missionaries from Britain and the United States, wonderful friends whose opinions I greatly respected.

However, some provided strong positive influences. My "American mother" Ruth Dietrich mentioned approvingly in a letter that a member of the Aurora church was running for city council, and commented that political involvement by Christian leaders increases positive influence. Another friend, Florence Christie, sent a tape with almost the same message.

93

Neither Ruth nor Florence knew anything about the decision we faced. Did they represent the voice of the Lord? The problems of the Palestinians weighed heavily on us. Would municipal office increase my influence for our cause?

We had to grapple with some harsh realities in deciding: We were in an occupied territory, and no Arab on the West Bank could vote or run for anything except the local municipal elections. I had no illusions about making a major impact. Public office made one vulnerable—on the one hand to the military government, and on the other to Palestinian constituents who might hope for more than I could deliver. Still, this seemed an opportunity for service.

For one thing, I could witness for Jesus Christ. As a member of the city council, I would be close to community leaders. Political participation might make me more effective with young people who needed positive role models. Nine years had passed since the war. A generation was emerging whose entire orientation came as victims of the military occupation. Some young people were apathetic; many were bitter. Both attitudes grieved me. Maybe, through Jesus' nonviolent principles, I could inspire them to work for solutions in positive rather than counterproductive ways.

Patricia influenced me the most. In reality we shared the decision. Although wives in Mideast culture stay in the background, some, like Pat, exert considerable influence on their husbands. She agreed with me that in our Israeli-dominated society Arabs should have a voice, and in our Moslem-dominated society Christians should have a voice. Perhaps I had a double obligation and opportunity.

We finally felt comfortable simply leaving it to God, with the vote as our guide: I entered my name with the understanding that if the Lord wanted me to serve, the sign would be a strong vote in the election. I told Mayor Khalaf that under those conditions I would run.

When they counted the votes, I was one of the nine elected to the council. With the second highest total, I became deputy mayor. The decision was clear and we felt good about it. I met with the council for business every Wednesday evening and consulted as needed throughout the week. Also, during the mayor's illness and injury I served as acting mayor, which required almost all my time. The office gave me an opportunity to help many people and share my concerns.

A few days after the 1976 election I led my first public demonstration. To consolidate their control, the Israelis had used an incident to try to drive a wedge between Moslem and Christian Arabs. So, holding a Bible in one hand and a Koran in the other, I appealed for solidarity to Christians and Moslems. We were united. I think my influence helped us to maintain the unified front that has never waned.

This political unity encouraged an important ministry for the Lord. Since then, many Moslems have asked me for Bibles. And I have had many opportunities to help people with their material and spiritual problems. A Moslem once asked me to look at his house. The wall had cracked from the floor to the ceiling. I told him that he had built his house on an inadequate foundation. He smiled and asked: "How did you know?" I responded: "If you hadn't, the wall wouldn't have cracked." Then I told him: "The Lord Jesus speaks about your case," and then I repeated Jesus' story about the wise man whose house on the rock withstood the storm, and the foolish man whose house on the sand crumbled (Matt. 7:24–27). I explained that Jesus was speaking of his life, and mine, and encouraged him to build his life on the firm foundation of Jesus Christ. Before he left, I referred him to the organization that could help repair the walls of his house.

In another incident while I was in office, about four hundred students, tired of Israeli control, walked out of their classes and came to the municipality to ask our help against the military. They wanted to quit school. I argued that this was exactly what the Israelis desired, because in ignorance we are more docile and easily divided—that we need education and solidarity. So the students went back to their classes.

On a similar occasion as I talked with students, the deputy military governor came into the room. He listened as I again explained that discontinuing schooling would only help the military government. They can use uneducated Arabs as a lower, laboring class that would benefit the occupation and impede our progress.

Afterward, the deputy governor told me: "You have no right to speak to people." I responded: "By whose orders do you say that?" "The military—my orders," he answered. "Well," I responded, "you are a military man. I am a clergyman. My attitude is the opposite of yours. Your government orders you to crush and oppress; my God calls me to lead and to guide." So he warned: "I'll put you in prison." I answered: "You can do whatever you want. You have the law in your hands. But I despise your uniform if it keeps you from being able to talk man-to-man and so come to some agreement and solution to these problems. The clothes put a barrier between us, concealing the importance of the person under them."

Although I did significant work for the city, it was somewhat routine. We provided administrative services, building permits, planning, and engineering for businesses. We maintained roads, supervised cleaning the town, and looked into violations of the law. With Palestinians lacking national representation, the municipal government tried to investigate imprisonments, speak out against atrocities, help people with other problems of the military occupation, and contact the Red Cross.

Until 1977 the Labour Party governed Israel. As the party of early Zionism, Labour formed the government that fought the Six Day War, established military control, and set up the settlement system that encouraged Jewish immigration to the West Bank. Then displaying an even harsher attitude, the Likud, the conservative party, came to power. Its leaders more adamantly enunciated their refusal to recognize that the West Bank existed, preferring to call it by the ancient Hebrew names of Judea and Samaria. This reminded me of an earlier prime minister, Golda Meir, who even insisted that there was no such thing as a Palestinian.

Life became even more difficult under the Likud. The government began to inaugurate what it called the "iron fist policy." In our Easter newsletter, 1980, Patricia wrote about its effects:

> The schools of Ramallah have been closed many days because of political reasons. There have been many strikes and protests against the policies of the government, and united support for students in prison without cause, or against the Israeli policy of confiscation of Arab land to build Jewish settlements. Yes, although we don't usually mention these things in our letters, people are suffering under occupation, with very little hope for the future. Children are living under pressure and fear, and it is only because of the sheer knowledge of Jesus as Lord and Savior and coming King that we can continue.

In May of 1980 the military authorities entered the homes of two mayors (Hebron and Halhoul). They blindfolded the men, took them to Lebanon, and expelled them.

A few days later, on Sunday evening, June 1, an unusual number of soldiers appeared in the streets of Ramallah. They went into the coffeehouses and other public buildings and ordered everyone out. Apprehension rose as the people returned to their homes. Later, a dentist friend told me that, while answering an emergency call at three o'clock the next morning, he saw a number of army vehicles parked sideways, blocking some major streets, including the one that led to the mayor's residence. Military personnel were everywhere.

That morning, when Mayor Khalaf tried to start his car, a bomb exploded and blew off his left foot and the calf of his right leg. The explosion jammed the left door, but he managed to throw himself out the right side moments before another blast destroyed the entire car. We then knew why the military had parked vehicles in the streets during the night: to prevent any uprisings that might result from the attack on the mayor.

The same morning a bomb exploded in the car of Mayor Shaka of Nablus, blowing away both his legs. (Shaka's daughter later recalled that when she ran to her father's side, a soldier handed her one of her father's bleeding legs, sardonically commenting: "Here. You may need this.") Someone who learned what was happening warned Mayor Taweel of El Bireh, making him suspicious. When soldiers told him to check his car, he refused. An officer then ordered a Druse soldier to investigate the car. Unfortunately, he obeyed, and received the full brunt of the explosion. It blinded him.

Late that night an ominous telephone call awakened us. When I sleepily took the phone, I heard: "You be quiet! Your turn is next!" Late the following Sunday night another caller pronounced: "You are a dead man." Later, several similar callers threatened me.

The intimidation was upsetting, but I felt as I had when I needed money in Wales, or protection in the Sudan, or when facing guns in Ramallah. My trust remained planted in God, the leader of my life. I took reasonable precautions, but I knew I must never be afraid to do his will. I had gone beyond fear. I would do whatever he asked and leave my protection to him.

If anything, the bombing and threats made me even more determined to work for Palestinian causes. When *Al-Fajr*, the Palestinian weekly newspaper, interviewed me three months later (September 1980), I made these points:

> This is our land. There won't be peace here unless the Israelis understand that the Palestinians have rights. . . .
>
> I call to the attention of our brothers, the Jews, that they should imagine themselves in our place. We do not want this state of belligerency. We do not want to continue this state of hatred. The sooner we sit down and try to reconcile our problems the better. The Israelis should wipe out of their minds that we, the Palestinians, want to kill them or drive them out. On the contrary, we want them to continue to work for peace. We want them to get to know us as people who have the right to live as they have the right to live.
>
> Let all of us have God's fear in our hearts. Let us have God's justice in our hearts because peace should be based on justice and mutual respect, not on confiscation of lands, imprisonment or oppression. As for world public opinion, I say peace in America and Europe and elsewhere will be based on peace in the Middle East. Everyone should work for peace and justice for the Palestinians.[1]

In our January 1981 newsletter Patricia looked back on the preceding year's trials:

> Nineteen-eighty was an especially busy year for Audeh, without vacations, as he has been acting Mayor of Ramallah since June 2nd. That was the day when our mayor was the victim of a bomb attack, leaving him seriously injured. In the same week, Audeh, himself, received threats on his life, but has not been intimidated—because of his deep faith in God. For the past six months he has been restricted in his movements, not being allowed to leave Ramallah on military orders.

During this period, many opportunities have been given to distribute God's Word to journalists and businessmen. We trust that soon the Mayor will be fit enough to take over his responsibilities, and that Audeh be allowed his freedom.

I acted as deputy mayor for three years. As Pat mentioned in our newsletter, the military authorities put me under "town arrest" for more than twelve months. They confined me strictly to Ramallah and refused to let me drive for about six months. If I had driven the car at all, or gone outside Ramallah, they undoubtedly would have imprisoned me.

During that time I often asked others to drive for me. The army kept close watch. Once they stopped us, surrounded the car with guns drawn and interrogated me, even though they could see I was not driving. The officer in charge asked: "Whose car is this?" I replied: "The church's." "Whom does the church allow to drive it?" "Anyone who has a license, and this young man has a license." "And who are you?" I responded: "If you did not know who I am you wouldn't have stopped me!" The officer backed off and let us continue.

Meanwhile, the military authorities continued to press for greater control. They detained Mayor Shaka and Mayor Khalaf one day in 1982. After reading a list of accusations, threatening expulsion, and grilling them for several hours, they released both men.

Mayor Khalaf then came directly to our house. This attracted the attention of newsmen and television crews. Soon our home seemed like a news center. This drew the attention of the military, who wanted to stop the newsmen from interviewing the mayor. As we ate dinner, we noticed tanks and soldiers surrounding our house.

The telephone rang. On the line was the deputy military governor, who asked for the mayor. He demanded that Mayor Khalaf leave immediately and report to the military coordinator in Jericho. Forced to obey, the mayor left, and soldiers followed him all the way to Jericho. They required him to stay there under town arrest and military guard for about a year, denying him some of the medical attention needed for his injury. The military also deported several other local Palestinian leaders—taking them to the border of Lebanon or across the river into Jordan with only the clothes on their backs, and ordering them never to return.

The military governor canceled the 1980 elections in nearly all West Bank and Gaza Strip jurisdictions, then two years later suspended those in office. Since 1982 Israel has appointed virtually all mayors, in order to govern through cooperative local leaders. (Palestinians living in Israel proper can vote and enjoy many of the rights of the Jewish citizenship. These comments about elections apply only to the occupied territories of the West Bank and Gaza Strip.)

In allowing local elections in 1976 the Israelis predicted that 70 percent would favor pro-Israeli candidates. They were mistaken. The ballot provided an opportunity to rally for our own causes and agitate for freedom. Therefore, since 1982 the military government has appointed only "loyal" local officers. We can no longer vote.

These actions constituted a general military crackdown, an attempt to enforce a stricter, harsher, more absolute control. The Zionists wanted sheep without a shepherd. They attempted to expel and deport the indigenous leadership and intimidate the rest of us into docility. They also tried to destroy the Palestine Liberation Organization (PLO), which we look to as our government in exile.

Thus the Israelis attempted to deny us both local and national leadership. It has not worked. For the occupiers it only made matters worse.

chapter eight

On June 6, 1982 (exactly fifteen years after Israeli troops entered Ramallah), Israel invaded Lebanon. They hoped to crush the Palestine Liberation Organization, part of which was in southern Lebanon. The Israelis reasoned that by destroying the PLO, the Palestinian resistance to the occupation would also be destroyed. According to historian Amos Perlmutter, Prime Minister Begin

> saw the Lebanon operation as his crowning achievement. . . . Begin probably envisioned the strike as ensuring that he could be the prime minister who, by destroying the PLO, created a secure and united Eretz Israel [greater Israel, expanded to include all of ancient Israel]. Sharon [defense minister] probably saw himself riding in triumph like some Roman praetor entering Jerusalem, the next king of Israel. . . .
>
> Israel, strong, secure, unchallenged as the most powerful military state in the Middle East, became enmeshed in a no-win, debilitating war. . . .[2]

Over the years southern Lebanon had become the refugee home for more than two hundred thousand Palestinians, most living in squalor and bitter resentment. Two camps, Sabra and Shantila, caught the brutal force of the insane war. In two bloody days Lebanese right-wing Phalangist troops, with the acquiescence of their Israeli allies, massacred at least fourteen hundred (some reports said as many as three thousand) Palestinian refugees. Most victims were women, children, and the aged. Upon hearing the news, I felt nauseated, recalling again the dark horror of Israel's Deir Yassin atrocity.

The parallel is overwhelming: In 1948 Menachem Begin, the master terrorist, applauded massacres that opened the door to the conquest of Palestine. In 1982 Menachem Begin, the prime minister, invaded Lebanon and opened the door to the massacres at Sabra and Shantila.

In some respects, the savage tragedies equate. Strangely, though, world reaction had changed. In 1948 the few who were aware merely winced, turned their faces, and called Deir Yassin's two hundred-fifty killings lamentable but probably necessary—a kind of necessary "collateral damage." In 1982 the Zionist state, scorned by many as just another aggressive nation, all but dissipated its reservoir of international good will. For the first time a disgusted world considered holding Israel accountable for its actions.

The invasion of Lebanon involved much more than Sabra and Shantila. The virtual destruction of Lebanon, including the two hundred forty-one dead United States marines in Beirut, and the spreading of fundamentalist Moslem fires, all proved counter to the interests of Israel and her allies. These failures closed the door on Menachem Begin's significant contribution to the Zionist conquests. Historian Amos Perlmutter makes a perceptive comment:

> Like a figure out of Greek tragedy, Begin at the end of 1983 disappeared into a self-imposed oblivion and exile. For an activist like Begin, this was doubly tragic and ironic. This true believer in the exclusivity of military power was undone, along with his ideological associates, by the greatest war Israel has ever participated in—a war he had helped plan and instigate. The war in Lebanon toppled the Begin myth and spirit, if not the Begin government. Begin's folly led to his inglorious resignation. . . .
>
> The domestic implications of the Lebanon war . . . left the nation leaderless, unfulfilled, and bitterly divided.[3]

Fear-driven, Isael still gropes in the dark, indiscriminately smashing Palestinian lives. Sometimes their mindless conduct affects those we love dearly.

In 1986 and again in 1987 the authorities arrested a close friend of our family, a young man who was eighteen in 1987. Each time they imprisoned him for eighteen days with no formal charge, refusing him permission to contact his family or an attorney. The officers tried to get him to admit membership in a political organization in his high school, or at least to participation in a demonstration. I will quote the story as he told it to me in 1987:

Just like last year, they arrested me at examination time. This means that once again I was unable to complete the tests, and so I will never be able to go to college or get a good job. I cannot go back to school again, because I have completed my years of high school. I could prepare for next year's test if I had enough money to hire someone to tutor me until I was ready again, but I don't think it would make any difference, because the soldiers told me that if I try to take the exam next year they will arrest me again. A lot of my classmates got arrested, too. We hadn't done anything illegal, but the Israelis think they can scare Palestinian kids out of giving them any trouble by accusing some people and then punishing them.

While in jail we all sat on the floor for several hours, with handcuffs and blindfolds on. The soldiers would walk by and kick our legs. Then they made us stand for 24 hours straight, all night and all day. After that they took me into a separate room, and the officer questioned me again:

"Do you want a drink?" "No."

"Do you want coffee?" "No."

"Do you want water?" "No."

"Why did you come here?" "I don't know. You brought me here."

"You mean you don't know?" "No."

"Look, I don't want to play around with you. You must tell us the information about the politics at the school." "I don't know about politics. I am not active at school."

Then he became very angry and threw coffee in my face, and said that if I didn't tell him about the school activities they would kill me. I didn't know what to say. Then he got another soldier and they took me into another room with a wheel and pulley overhead. They tied my hands and stretched my arms up, then made me climb onto a barrel and kicked it out from under me. I hung there for a long time. It probably was only ten minutes, but it seemed like an hour.

While I was dangling from the ceiling, thinking my arms would come out of the sockets, one of the soldiers climbed up and put his lighted cigarette against my wrists, over and over, not trying to put it out but just to let it burn into my skin. Oh that hurt! Then they let me down and finally put me in solitary confinement, where I stayed for six days, except two hours each day when they brought me out for interrogation. Finally, they put me into a room with an old man, a college professor who was in prison for writing a book that told the truth about the way Israelis treat Palestinians.

They released me after eighteen days. The jailer told me I had stood firmly, but they had ways and means to break me down, and said if I didn't talk they would make sure I never had a chance to take the school examinations. That was when he told me that if I tried to take the exam next year, they would arrest me again.

My young friend had correctly analyzed the purpose: to intimidate younger people to be docile. The policy is failing, however. The harsher the treatment, the deeper the resentment. For years my young friend has borne the scars from those cigarette burns. The scars on his soul will last forever.

This young friend spent much time in our home before and after his arrests. Imprisonment left him with a blood disease; he became desperately ill, lost the sight in one eye, and almost died. He is a Moslem who had lived with his family in a nearby refugee camp. I am overjoyed to report that he recently accepted Jesus Christ as his personal Savior.

This eighteen-year-old's experience reminds me that at eighteen I had the opportunity to go to college. I live a satisfying life and make some contribution to those around me, partially as a result of that education. Since the examinations are prerequisites to further education and good employment, the authorities have severely limited my friend's potential.

It is sad that since 1967 they have denied many other young people education and hope. Caught in a helpless dilemma and subjected to conditions that naturally produce enormous resentment, these young Palestinians gain self-respect by working courageously for our national freedom.

Another bizarre tactic has also become common. Israel increasingly uses collective punishment to intimidate the families of "troublemakers." I will cite three somewhat typical examples.

In 1987 the military dynamited a Ramallah house in reprisal against an Israeli bus explosion four years earlier. Frustrated by failure to catch the accused young man, the authorities bombed his parents' home. A year later they indiscriminately dynamited fourteen Arab houses in retaliation for a young Jewish girl's death. Incorrectly assuming that Palestinians had killed her, Israeli settlers, like a mindless lynch mob, destroyed the people's homes. On one occasion near Ramallah, settlers accused Palestinians of burning one of their buses and promptly bulldozed a nearby olive grove.

Such collective punishment reflects the theory that if sufficiently frightened, people will keep their children and neighbors submissive to military authority. It makes no real difference who is guilty. They just try to prevent the problem from recurring. One Palestinian is as good as another when they need an example.

Deportation permanently rends people's homes, making it perhaps the worst punishment. The usual procedure resembles the Nazi Gestapo's seizure of Jews for the concentration camps: The military police come after midnight, surround the house, and arrest the victim. The next morning we learn they have deported our friend. We can appeal only to the indifferent, compassionless Israeli military officials. The refusal of local autonomy, the tragedy of Lebanon, and the general military crackdown have rapidly moved us toward bloodshed.

My political involvement brought me face-to-face with many Jews, sharpening my understanding of their insecurities. The increasing hostilities gave rise to another worry—a kind of twin to my concern for my fellow Palestinians. I fear erosion of the compassion that the world holds for Jews. The stench of the gas chambers made anti-Semitism repulsive to all mankind. Who could not cry out in empathetic disgust and guilt for the misery caused by unreasoning fear and hatred? Now, as the world ponders and questions Israel's harsh occupation, that reservoir of sympathy dissipates. How tragic if in their compulsion for security, the Zionists open the door to another dread wave of mindless anti-Semitism.

I pray that God will protect my Jewish friends from racist, expansionist Zionism and world reaction to it. Some faithfully practice Judaism; others deny the faith of their fathers. Those who have found the Messiah, Jesus, are the closest to me. Christian Jews, along with gentile believers, are true sons of Abraham. All Christians embody the real Israel, the Israel of God.

I attended an international Christian conference in Athens in 1983. The participants included some Jewish Christians who never had met any Arab Christians, and some Arab Christians who never had met any Christian Jews. The mutual struggle for understanding brought growth as we knelt together at the foot of the cross, where ethnic divisions disappear in the light of our Lord's presence. Fellowship has continued since that meeting, with Jewish and Arabic Christians convening regularly. As one speaker pronounced, "We come together on the basis of Calvary. Christ is our common denominator." Even political disagreements, the iron fist, and the intifada, have not separated our communion nor interrupted our meetings. Our gatherings still reflect the shared love of our Redeemer.

I also enjoy friendships with non-Christian Jews, especially those who oppose the occupation. We sometimes meet to find ways to work together as Arabs and Jews. As deputy mayor, I developed some relationships with Jews in the military occupation. I once felt led to tell the military governor and his deputy: "You say that the Messiah will be coming. We also believe he is coming, but for the second time. The problem with you is that like people going to the train station, you arrived too late and missed the train. You had better catch up." I had similar contacts with other Jewish officers; on one occasion I addressed forty colonels and three generals. I was able to develop cordial, although not deep, friendships with some of these people.

As deputy mayor I established no real friendships with the West Bank Jewish settlers. As the first wave of Zionist expansion, they view themselves as pioneers in hostile territory. They express hard-line, antagonistic attitudes, and consider Palestinians as nothing but impediments to the progress of the "superior" people. Palestinians resent their arrogance and their unquestioning assumption that they have the right to the West Bank. Obviously, hospitality is difficult.

However, at the time of the Feast of Tabernacles, when Jews search for palm branches for their worship, I provide some from our palm tree. I find it hard to be Christlike with them, but while consistently combatting their occupation, I try to develop congenial relationships.

I will always be glad that I became active in the municipality. Office-holding increased my burdens but multiplied my opportunities. I feel that all people—Arabs, Jews, and those from the outside world—should cooperate toward a peaceful end to the terrible insecurity imposed on the Palestinians. I remain dedicated to influencing others toward this goal.

Intifada

I NTIFADA! The uprising. More accurately, it is the "shaking off" of an undesirable substance, as an animal shakes off dust or a parasite. Palestinians have had enough of occupation. They have decided to get rid of it.

In one sense we feel like Jesus' early followers. He sent them out to witness, and instructed them to shake the dust from their feet when people would not listen.

Long before the intifada began in late 1987, Palestinians knew they were moving toward a precipice. We teetered between total subjugation by Israel and all-out confrontation against them. With our grievances underestimated by Israel and unrecognized by casual visitors, we struggled for justice.

After the beginning of Israel's iron fist policy in 1980, we lived with a gradually rising fever. It was like a tightly capped pressure cooker steaming inside—gradually building toward explosion. In December of 1987 it erupted into *intifada*.

The conservative Israeli government reacted in the only way it knew. It struggled to hold down the lid, tightening its grip, and buttressing the military. In so doing it only exacerbated the problem—it raised the fever, it increased the pressure within the cooker. Then, like most authoritarian governments, it blamed outside agitators for the explosion its own policies had provoked.

Palestinians in the occupied territories responded in the

only way they could: They forcefully shook, determined to rid themselves of the intruder.

Palestinian Davids face the Israeli Goliath. The Davids now walk beyond fear of the Israeli evil, through the dark valley of the shadow of death, unified as never before, exuding a new determination and a renewed sense of personal and national dignity. The giant retaliates with the sword—rubber and metal bullets, dynamite and bulldozer, bashing young heads into the "wall of blood" in Ramallah, abortion-inducing tear gas, deportations, imprisonment with neither formal charge nor legal recourse, and by denying education to our children.

We are in a revolution. When remembering the French and Russian revolutions, the mind is filled with thoughts of savage violence. Intifada is different. It springs from within as a united attitude that does not depend on weapons. This revolutionary movement can neither conquer nor be suppressed by violence.

When did it start? When does any revolution start? One searches fruitlessly for the exact moment because rebellion grows from the grievances of many decades. *The spark that ignites causes no explosion unless the powder keg of discontent is full and overflowing.*

Nevertheless, every uprising produces a critical moment between indecision and action. This one sparked to life in December of 1987 when on the Gaza Strip, an Israeli truck slammed into two Palestinian cars. Four died and seventeen were wounded (an indiscriminate reprisal for the stabbing of an Israeli soldier, military reports suggested). As with similar incidents, the authorities gave the Israeli driver only a traffic citation. Palestinians protested and the military characteristically moved in with brute force. Protests spread, women joined in the demonstrations, and children attached themselves to the cause with little concern for their lives. The almost spontaneously ignited intifada became therapy for two decades of affliction.

This situation reminds me of Rosa Parks, a black American arrested in 1955. After a lifetime as a victim, she finally rejected the indignity of having to sit in the back of the city bus. Sickened by a lifetime of dehumanizing racism, she wanted recognition as a person. Just as long-smoldering resentment erupted into America's black revolution, Palestinian despair turned into action in 1987. From the bottom of their hearts our people cried out for respect.

Palestinian moral outrage has grown through the centuries: the foul fruits of the Ottoman oppression, bitterness with British betrayal, fear of Zionist aggression—each has played its part. We on the West Bank experienced some anti-Jordanian feelings from 1949–67. To Israel's occupation in 1967 we reacted with a sharply intensified nationalism. Later the Likud government broadened the settlement policy, imposed the crackdowns of 1980, deposed elected local leaders from office, and invaded Lebanon. All this made intifada inevitable.

Israel's insecurity is understandable, given their victimization throughout history. They have suffered dehumanization and treatment as nonpersons. Yet who better than they should identify with the deep inner longing for freedom, the desire to have one's own nation? Who better than they should recognize that enforced indignity embitters the victim and prompts retaliation? Persistent dehumanization burns in every Palestinian consciousness and calls out for redemption. Jews should understand.

In earlier chapters I discussed Israel's policy regarding the occupied territories. Now I will give a few recent examples of Israeli actions that, although used persistently since 1967, take on special significance when trying to identify causes for uprisings.

Some reflect Israel's official disdain for Palestinian dignity. For example, during house-to-house searches authorities occasionally attempt to force a Palestinian into acts of self-derogation. They punish those who refuse to obey.

Palestinians resent the heavy taxation without representation, which sometimes includes fines in addition to regular taxes. Israel has continued to flaunt its power through curfews, property confiscation, town arrests, administrative detention (imprisonment without formal charge or trial), collective punishment, deportation, school closures, and other forms of intimidation. I will comment on only a few of these.

As early as 1984 Amnesty International studied the town arrests and verified the obvious. The report noted that those arrested included "mayors (who were dismissed from office in 1981–82), journalists, doctors, lawyers, trade unionists, teachers, writers and students (many of them members of university student councils)." Israeli authorities argued in rebuttal that "no one is subjected to town arrest orders because of non-violent exercise of their right to freedom of opinion and expression."[1]

I know for a fact, however, that many peace-loving people have faced town arrest. I, as one of those arrested, seek to emulate Jesus' nonviolent example. The authorities arrest many others who share my convictions. Most Israelis feel threatened even by peaceful resistance to official will.

Sometimes military law is enforced against large groups, but they often enforce it against individuals or families. The family of a dear Gazan friend has suffered for years. Their suffering intensified during the intifada.

Our friendship goes back to the late '60s when I met him selling colored woven carpets in the streets of Ramallah. He had several carpets flung over his arm and was haggling over the price. We needed floor rugs to lay over the cold, bare tile, so I told him "I will give you a good price for all the rugs on the condition that you deliver them to my house."

When the rugs were duly delivered, I invited him in and served coffee. His eyes kept wandering to my bookshelves, and I asked him if he could read. He surprised me by revealing that he had read many classical, Arabic books. However, as a Moslem, he had never read the Bible, so he asked to borrow one. Taking it, he asked to come back with a list of questions. This was the beginning of a beautiful friendship. We often conversed about important questions of politics and personal faith.

Later, he became ill with tuberculosis, but one day he managed to leave the hospital and come to Ramallah. He asked for some more New Testaments, in order to share biblical truth with other patients. The doctor later expressed amazement that all the patients were reading Scripture.

After this dear brother's recovery, he invited us to his home in Gaza. We enjoyed a bountiful feast and wonderful fellowship. Sadly, he was a tormented man when I met him again in 1988. He arrived at our home greatly agitated, looking tired and haggard, his tall body stooped and bent, looking much older than his years.

I greeted him with the usual enthusiastic hugs that men exchange in the Middle East. "*Ahlan Wa Sahlan,* Welcome! How nice to see you after such a long time. How are you?"

Nearly in tears he told how eight members of his family had suffered because they had distributed leaflets in support of the intifada. Soldiers had entered my friend's refugee camp home in the middle of the night, dragged every member out of bed, and beaten them with clubs. His wife had to go to the hospital because of internal bleeding. Soldiers beat one of the older sons until his arms were broken, then made him stand up to his neck in a pit of mud.

My friend refused to stay for a meal or even a cup of coffee. However, he did accept a sack of used clothing to distribute among the needy in the refugee camp. His wife died several weeks later.

Along with fellow Palestinians, we face the iron fist, determined to resist. We persevere in spite of deep emotional pain. And Patricia never seems to regret her decision to join me. Early in the intifada, on February 8, 1988, she mentioned some of our hardships in our newsletter:

> Loving greetings from Ramallah!
>
> We want you to know how very much your cards and letters have been appreciated. Thank you for showing a prayerful concern in our troubled situation. We really need your prayers and support at this time.
>
> No doubt you have been following the news and wonder if it is all true. We can assure you that every Palestinian family is suffering during the present uprising. When you take away the identity and self-respect of a people, is it any wonder they try to revolt? And what can a handful of children throwing stones do to one of the most powerful armies in the world?
>
> We could write page after page of the unjust sufferings of our people. Those who get beaten or shot even try to avoid the hospital register; it means sure arrest and imprisonment. Then there are the Jewish settlers who destroy property and kidnap young people, even sometimes burying them alive.
>
> And what about the Christian Palestinians? Many tourists are not aware of the living Church, existing here since the time of Jesus. That is why *we* are here; to educate Christian Palestinian boys, to encourage them to hold fast to their faith, to be witnesses and a help in the community, and to stick fast to their culture and identity.
>
> In our household, none of us have suffered physical injuries, but our car (the Talbot) was completely destroyed by someone who deliberately set fire to it. It happened Feb. 1st around

8:00 P.M., just as it was parked in our back yard. We still have the Austin car, as Audeh was out at the time.

All schools are closed, so most of the children are away with relatives. There are 7 boys with us right now.

We do not know why they destroyed our car. We learned that a man who collaborates with the military authorities set it ablaze. That particular night it stormed, with torrential rain accompanied by thunder and lightning. Suddenly, one of our staff saw the flames from a back window and shouted "Fire, Fire!" Another staff member thought the house was on fire, so quickly aroused all our boys. The car exploded before the police and fire brigade arrived.

Incidents happen regularly. For example, soldiers in a jeep stopped in front of the Catholic church and attacked my friend, Father Faisal. They accused him of demonstrating. So, the next day pastors of all the Ramallah churches demonstrated. I marched down the street arm in arm with Father Faisal, carrying a sign announcing: THE WORLD IS WATCHING. WHAT IS IN US IS IN US. The soldiers watched us carefully, with their guns ready, but this time they did not interfere.

One day Pat and our daughter Hilary marched with several hundred women and girls in a nonviolent demonstration. Some carried the forbidden Palestinian flag. "When we arrived in the center of the town," Pat told me, "the army fired tear gas. We all carried onions or lemons to smell, and it helped. Then they fired rubber bullets (which have steel in the middle). Hilary and I retreated a safe distance and avoided injury. However, bullets hit several of our neighbor women, and the soldiers beat some of them with clubs."

The next day Patricia wrote the following poem:

> Blood, struggle, fun?
> Exhilaration, who won?

Green, black, white and red or
Blue and white with six points?

Once the oppressed, the smell of ovens,
The black twisted cross, the hate,
The love, desolation of late years forgotten?
Now the Oppressor?

Is it nothing to you
All you that pass by,
He bore our guilt, His bitter wine
Became our Eucharist, for me and mine.

We will always commemorate November 15, 1988, the most momentous day in Palestinian history—the day on which we declared independence. Centuries from now that date will live for us, like July 4, 1776, for Americans. The announcement brought great joy and celebration. Ecstatic crowds marched on that momentous day.

Israel multiplied its troop strength in Ramallah. The army threatened five years' imprisonment for setting off sparklers or firecrackers, or for showing our green, black, white, and red flag. The demonstration continued anyway, with multitudes dancing in the streets and shouting for joy.

The government took me to headquarters for questioning and accused me of ringing the church bells. All the churches had agreed to ring their bells at an appointed time that morning. I told the military interrogator that we had been waiting forty years for these church bells!

A few days later the military interrogated me again. Each time they held me for several hours, seeking to harass and intimidate me. The military men represented a government that had used terrorism to win Israeli independence in 1948 and to take three-fourths of Palestine. Yet they had the gall to label the PLO, my government in exile, a terrorist organization and to say that therefore I should not support independence! That made me very angry.

Patricia tells of her experiences on independence day:

> Many of the women and girls of Ramallah danced in the streets, waving Palestinian flags, whirling their scarfs in the air, singing, and clapping in a joyous celebration. It was like a Palestinian wedding. Many of the old women were making a cry of joy like they do at weddings—they call it *zaghared,* a shout peculiar to Arabs. It was beautiful.
>
> Then the army came and shot tear gas canisters. All the women ran into their homes until the soldiers had driven around the corner. Then we came out again, singing and clapping. It happened again and again. The cat-and-mouse game went on all morning, until finally some of the girls got tired of it and just stayed out when the soldiers drove up in their jeeps.
>
> The soldiers stopped. The girls said: "Why are you playing games with us like this? Why are you shooting the tear gas?" They didn't give very good answers, but were quite congenial. Actually, they responded politely. So did we. After that they just went away and let us continue to celebrate.

Often, however, the incidents get ugly and dangerous. Almost every day we in Ramallah experience a few minutes in which someone challenges the soldiers' authority by putting tire barricades into the streets, or by throwing rocks. The soldiers frequently retaliate by shooting rubber or live bullets. Pat tells of one typical example:

> As we approached our church on Christmas day (1988) we saw young people putting a barricade across the street. The army came, and some boys and girls threw stones. We could see that the soldiers were starting to shoot at the children, so we retraced our steps and took a side road to the church. Then we hid behind a wall and waited several minutes. When the fighting died down, we ran quickly into the church and enjoyed the Lord's presence, in spite of the circumstances.

Another day not long afterward we couldn't leave church because of a battle outside. Incidents like this are very common.

One day in 1989 our boys and the children from the girls' home studied the parable of the good shepherd. Their teacher decided to take them into the valley nearby to visit a modern-day shepherd with his sheep. Coming back, they encountered some Jewish settlers. The settlers got out of their car and began shooting in the air. Panicking, our children ran in different directions.

A settler ordered one of the boys into his car. Out of fear, the child obeyed. The settler put him on the back floor, under the feet of the car's other occupants, and drove to the settlement. The terrified children ran to our house; the kidnapped boy's brother cried uncontrollably.

I immediately drove to the settlement, not far from where we live. For a long time they kept me at the gate, the guards refusing to admit they had our boy. Eventually, however, they acknowledged that he had been taken to the military governor.

I went to the governor's office. After I appealed, they released him to me, but required that he return the next morning. Todd Hicks, my assistant, went with him. When they tried to force the boy to sign a paper saying he had thrown stones, Todd demanded the name of the settler who had made the accusation. They refused to tell, but finally did let the boy go.

Although frightened and bruised from the blows and kicks of the settlers, he was not seriously hurt—physically. However, the experience did damage to my hope that he might someday become an agent of loving, peaceful reconciliation.

Although I face massive obstacles, I continue my task— trying to teach my boys that neither side can win by dehumanizing the other. Neither can win by defeating the other in bloody conquest. Fortunately, many Israelis teach their children the same thing.

I hope public opinion will influence the authorities by helping them comprehend the enormous cost of their policies. Israel's economic losses are staggering—the first three months of the intifada alone cost them an estimated three hundred million[2]—but the losses in public relations and world confidence are far more significant.

Some Israeli Jews counsel against the West Bank and Gaza policy. For example, a massive protest demonstration in Tel Aviv attracted at least fifty thousand people. A number of Jewish organizations have formed to challenge the military policy.

Yehoshafat Harkabi, a retired general and head of Israeli intelligence, speaks out for change. In 1988 he warned:

> We will have to negotiate with the Palestinians, the majority of whom, in any referendum, would vote for the PLO as their representative, not out of love, but as the unparalleled symbol of the idea that the Palestinians are a human public worthy of political expression. The U.S. does not determine the composition of the Soviet delegation to negotiations, and Israel's presumption in trying to determine the composition of the Arab delegation is an absurdity bound to fail.[3]

The government's policies also make Jews outside Israel apprehensive. In 1988, *Los Angeles Times* pollsters discovered that 29 percent of all U.S. Jews favor establishing a Palestinian national homeland in the occupied territories.[4]

Michael Lerner, Jewish editor of *Tikkun* magazine, calls the occupation of the West Bank and Gaza Strip "immoral and stupid." Following are a few of his thoughts:

> The pain and sorrow many American Jews feel about Israel's policies on the West Bank and Gaza are rooted deep in our

collective memory as a people. Israel's attempt to regain control of the refugee camps by denying food to hundreds of thousands of men, women, and children, by raiding homes and dragging out their occupants in the middle of the night to stand for hours in the cold, by savagely beating a civilian population and breaking its bones—these activities are deplorable to any civilized human being. *That they are being done by a Jewish state is both tragic and inexcusable.* We did not survive the gas chambers and crematoria so that we could become the oppressors of Gaza. The Israeli politicians who have led us into this morass are desecrating the legacy of Jewish history. If Jewish tradition has stood for anything, it has stood for the principle that justice must triumph over violence. For that reason, we typically have sided with the oppressed and have questioned the indiscriminate use of force. We, who love Israel, who remain proud Zionists, are outraged at the betrayal of this sacred legacy by small-minded Israeli politicians who feel more comfortable with the politics of repression than with the search for peace.

Any policy that requires the immoral tactics currently being used against an unarmed and militarily subjugated population must be rejected.[5]

Lerner also argues that an end to occupation would promote Israeli self-interest because prolonged control will further ignite Palestinians in both the occupied territories and Israel. In response, the military will become more repressive, anti-Semitism will increase, and in the United States, popular support for Israel will erode. He continues:

A Judaism that has lost its moral teeth and becomes an apologist for every Israeli policy, no matter what its moral content, is a Judaism that not only betrays the prophetic tradition, but also risks losing the adherence of the Jewish people.[6]

Many non-Jews also criticize Israeli policy. For example, the *Los Angeles Times* poll cited earlier revealed that half of

U.S. non-Jews favor a Palestinian state. The British Minister of State for Foreign Affairs called a refugee camp he visited "an affront to civilized values."[7] Amnesty International sharply criticized the iron fist policy and called for an investigation into "extensive" human rights violations. Its head of research reported:

> Questions must be answered about central government encouragement of punitive or deterrent beatings, the legality of orders to soldiers and the adequacy of established methods of investigating reports of abuses. Piecemeal investigations by the IDF [Israeli Defense Force] would not suffice.[8]

The organization recommended investigation of reports that soldiers enter homes at night and arrest people indiscriminately, sometimes including all teenagers. Amnesty International also charged that authorities have arrested children as young as twelve, and have held many in "incommunicado detention" for up to two weeks. Hundreds have received from twenty days to thirty months in prison for throwing stones and gasoline bombs, burning tires, or participating in illegal demonstrations. (I can acknowledge from personal observation that such actions *have* taken place; in fact, this was occurring repeatedly before the intifada, but then hardly any outsiders noticed.) Such reports raise awareness of the situation and help us move toward freedom.

Above the critical voices of Jews and non-Jews throughout the world, I hear voices right here at home. Raja Shehadeh, a Ramallah lawyer, eloquently speaks for our cause. Several years ago he wrote beautifully of "the third way": "Between mute submission and blind hate I choose the third way. I am *Simud*." ("Simud" means "the steadfast, the persevering.") Shehadeh tells of his deep friendship with Enoch, a Jew:

> Enoch's mother, whom he adored, was a fervent Zionist. When she died, he came to Israel to carry out her dream. He

did not like what he saw—he regarded much of modern Israel as a betrayal of what he valued in Judaism. But he did not feel free to walk away, because he saw the relations between Jews and Arabs as the moral test that Judaism must pass. I think that this is our deepest bond—our determination, on either side of the fence, to persist, not to pack up our bags and leave the land we love in the hands of those who are driving us to war.

Enoch does not expect me to forget, when we laugh and walk together, nor does he forget himself, the accumulation through the years of the wrongs that his people have done to mine . . . no more than I expect him to forget the terrible sufferings of his people. And here, too, Enoch's attitude is rare. Most well-meaning Israelis adopt a stance of "forgive and forget" on meeting samidin—but without any knowledge of what they are asking us to forget. They mean that we should forgive and forget things that they don't even bother to know about, things that happened to us because they came here.

It was because Enoch forgets neither his nor my people's suffering—without entering into an obscene competition of who suffered more—that I have learned from him to be open to, and feel deeply, the past history of the Jews and what Israel means to them. It is due to him that I have come to accept that the Palestinians will have to sacrifice a lot for peace: we will have to learn to share our land with the Jews in pre-'67 Israel—those who have settled in the Jaffa that my parents left and on land where whole villages of ours have been wiped out.

But there is something sadly paradoxical in my learning this from Enoch, because the deep trust I have in him, which made me see this, is the exception to the rule. And often there is a feeling about our friendship of time borrowed until we are each thrust into the role of being soldiers in the bloody war that will rage for a long time between our peoples.

Enoch once wrote to me: "When I think of Enoch, the individual, meeting Raja, the individual, I feel no tension. When I think of Enoch, the Jew, encountering Raja, the Palestinian, I feel the tension of conflict of interest, of history, of murder. At first I feel anger because the political situation may rob me of Raja my friend, because I can no longer meet him under these conditions, and because under these conditions my friend will cease to exist. But in more optimistic moods, I believe that I will be able to meet Raja, the Palestinian, as a friend and as a comrade. Yet, we are not masters of our own fate."

And it is this oscillation between hope and despair that hovers over the times we spend together.

It is hard by now to think that a political solution is going to work here—certainly not before much blood is spilt. Enoch speaks of the "demonic, subterranean" vengeance and fear that drive both of our peoples. And he wrote: "After so much suffering, killing, distrust—there need to be some rituals of truce, of mutual confessions of wrongdoing, so that a more genuine intimacy may grow on the seedbed of despair. In short, we must beg each other's forgiveness, and if people cannot come in their pride to humble themselves before one another, then perhaps we can all, in our own way but together, ask forgiveness of a higher power."

Enoch is religious in an unusual way, and he believes in this higher power. But I must make do with my belief in man; perhaps for that reason my despair is sometimes greater than his.

I have been with Enoch to Yad Vashem, the memorial for the six million Jews exterminated by the Nazis. It was there that Enoch taught me the wisdom of the inmates of the Treblinka concentration camp: "Faced with two alternatives, always choose the third."

Like many Palestinians, I used to see it as inevitable that the survivors of the holocaust would be driven by such hate and fear that they would act ruthlessly to ensure their own preservation, regardless of who paid for it. But Enoch remembers the evil perpetrated against his people, remembers it deeply, without himself being a hate-blinded, vengeance-seeking victim of that wrong. In him I see that really honouring the memory of people who have suffered creates courage and a capacity for love that cannot be equalled by someone who does not remember or acknowledge man's capacity for evil. What I have learned from Enoch has made

125

me expect more from the Jews—which is not easy because it opens a place for hope and its betrayal. But even more importantly, it has taught me to expect more of myself: never to excuse in myself the psychology of a victim—someone whose actions and reactions you can understand, in the circumstances, but not respect.

Enoch speaks much of the "third way." I am not sure I fully understand what it means to him, but I think that it is close to much I myself seek as Samid. For Enoch, I know that the third way is God's way—one which he must discover and follow in order to avoid being trapped into accepting the choice between two wrong alternatives. But I cannot think of it as God's path that is out there, beckoning, waiting to be discovered. It must, for me, be something that is created as I go along, forged step by step while I live here as Samid.

I think a lot about the choice that samidin feel cornered into making: exile or submissive capitulation to the occupation, on the one hand—or blind, consuming hate and avenging the wrongs done to them, on the other. But it is in this conception of choice that the trap lies. States of mind cannot be forced on you. This is where you are free, your own master—because your mind is the one thing that you can prevent your oppressor from having the power to touch, however strong and brutal he may be. If he has touched it, that is when you have been defeated, and that is when you become a predictable puppet, a bundle of psychological characteristics that the experts can study and use for their own purposes. I know that my Israeli occupiers want me in this state—want me to believe that vengeance and submission are my only alternatives. I know, too, that I am close to defeat when I feel driven by them, scarcely recognizing that these are their alternatives, not mine.

All of this is difficult to express and even more difficult, almost impossible to live by. But I must succeed in order to be Samid. For it is this freedom that is most vulnerable under the long-drawn-out occupation, with no end in sight but war. And even that end, which I dread, may take a long time in coming.

It is the day-to-day living that is the test of simud. And I know that I fail very often.[9]

So do I. Yet I pray that I can stay true to the God who empowers me to love my enemies and work for freedom.

Mubarak Awad also champions the "third way"—the alternative between blind obedience and blind rage.[10] Awad, a Christian, created the Palestinian Center for the Study of Nonviolence and wrote *Nonviolent Resistance: A Strategy for the Occupied Territories*. Espousing tactics similar to those of Mahatma Gandhi and Martin Luther King, Jr., Awad calls forthrightly for direct but nonviolent action against the occupation. He advocates methods such as boycotts and refusal to obey orders, while attaining the moral high ground by refusing to hate.

One midnight in the spring of 1988, eighteen men in plain clothes pounded on Mubarak Awad's door. Refusing to identify themselves, they entered his house and arrested him. The authorities jailed him for forty days, then deported him to the United States.[11] They charged him with being an alien because, although born in Jerusalem, he had resided in the United States and also had U.S. citizenship. The real provocation was that the military occupation cannot tolerate threats to its total control over the Palestinians. Mubarak Awad's nonviolent teachings scare the authorities because they do not know how to combat such tactics.

Father Elias Chacour stood on the mount overlooking the Sea of Galilee and experienced a profound spiritual and intellectual rebirth. This man of God, the Palestinian author of *Blood Brothers,* had discovered in Jesus' Sermon on the Mount (Matthew 5–7) a loving alternative to the twin sins of blind submission and blind rage:

One of the first things Jesus did when He reconciled man to God was to restore human dignity.

The reason Jesus' words had struck me was this: Suddenly I knew that the first step toward reconciling Jew and Palestinian was the restoration of human dignity. Justice and righteousness were what I had been hungering and thirsting for: This was the third choice that ran like a straight path between violent opposition and calcified, passive nonresistance. If I were really committing my life to carry God's message to my people, I would have to lift up, as Jesus had, the men and women who had been degraded and beaten down. Only by regaining their shattered human dignity could they begin to be reconciled to the Israeli people, whom they saw as their enemies. This, I knew at once, went beyond all claims of land and rightful ownership; it was the true beginning. . . .

If I was to go out as a true servant of God and man, my first calling was to be a peacemaker.[12]

Chacour found the key to personal victory over his hatred of the oppressor. On a night of personal rage and tragedy, he saw himself as in a dream, ready to commit the violence he hated in the enemy:

Silent, still, I lay there, aware for the first time that I was capable of vicious, killing hatred. Aware that all men everywhere—despite the thin, polite veneer of society—are capable of hideous violence against other men. Not just the Nazis, or the Zionists or the Palestinian commandos—but me. I had covered my hurts with Christian responses, but inside the anger had gnawed. With this sudden, startling view of myself, a familiar inner voice spoke firmly, without compromise: If you hate your brother you are guilty of murder. Now I understood.

I was aware of other words being spoken. A Man was dying a hideous death at the hands of His captors—a Man of Peace, who suffered unjustly—hung on a cross. *Father forgive them,* I repeated. *And forgive me, too.*

In that moment, forgiveness closed the long-open gap of anger and bitterness inside me. From the time I had been

beaten as a small boy, I had denied the violence inside me.
Now . . . the taming hand that had taught me compassion . . .
finally stilled me enough to see the deep hatred in my own
soul.[13]

Compassion—love—human dignity. These very powerful
words fill my soul and commit me to Jesus' way. He calls me
to live out his gospel, in his power to renounce the evil within
me, and seek freedom for my people.

Yet sometimes Israeli tactics almost make me despair,
because in my more depressed moments I fear that Israel will
never allow freedom except in the face of bloody revolution.
How can we avoid violence when they will not let us make
progress in any other way? Still, I believe that we must
continue to emulate those such as Martin Luther King, Jr.,
who believed unearned suffering is redemptive.

Sometimes we observe symbolic acts that make us hopeful.
Raja Shehadeh recalled one such incident:

> As I was driving back into Ramallah with Jonathan [Kuttab]
> this afternoon, we saw a jeep draw up near some boys who
> were playing football against a wall in old Ramallah. A few
> days earlier a schoolboy had been shot in the hand by a soldier
> driving by the same place. Our hearts sank as we saw a young
> soldier jump out of the jeep. The boys began to run—the ball
> was in mid-air. The soldier caught it, kicked it back at the
> fleeing boys who, after a split second of amazement, laughed,
> caught it and kicked it back at the soldier. We left them all
> playing football, laughing, shouting. I feel myself smiling as I
> sit here in my room with the picture of the soldier boy and the
> Arab boys suspended for a moment of peace in the soft
> twilight.[14]

"The soldier boy and the Arab boys." How true! I am
impressed by the youthfulness of the contenders here. Some
Jewish soldiers seem almost like boys and girls—many of
them are very young. They are much like Palestinian boys and

girls, except that in this dread relationship they have guns to protect the land that their parents told them should be theirs.

Many of these young soldiers patrolled Ramallah even before the intifada. They harass us from the rooftops, jeeps, everywhere. Yet as soldiers trained for battle, many suffer deep emotional scars as they beat and shoot unarmed men, women, and children. No one prepared them to trample innocent people.

Sometimes I pause and look at one of these young soldiers, pondering the person's background and future. I pray that God might perform his true will in that life, just as he did in mine at that age. The soldier's needs, hopes, and ambitions are exactly like those of our boys in the Evangelical Home. It makes one weep to see so much animosity among young people who should be kicking footballs together, not hating each other.

We endure a hard environment. In spite of the adversity, Patricia and I enjoy satisfying lives, with a real sense of accomplishment. We married in 1965 wanting to help dependent children. We had no idea that two years later military occupation would severely disrupt our lives. Nevertheless, God is fulfilling our dreams. We now have a home large enough for our own family and eighty needy boys.

Those boys—who are much like the young Jewish soldiers on the streets—provide us with an important and fulfilling vocation. We live in a political maelstrom, but gain our principal satisfaction from watching our large family develop. We encourage within them a personal relationship with the Lord, who can teach them to love, not loathe the soldiers who cause so much distress.

As with our public lives, we have dedicated our private lives to God's service. The next chapter tells the story of our immediate family and our work.

chapter ten

Work and Family

*M*Y *HUMAN* concern began when as an eleven-year-old refugee I saw thousands suffering and dying. It struck home when I began to understand John 3:16: God loved me and purchased my salvation; I was a worthy person, one whom Jesus Christ actually wanted to use.

With this insight, I accepted Christ in a very personal sense. The experience deepened two years later when I understood that the "whosoever" in that verse meant everyone. God called me to share his love with everyone I could.

I am glad that children are my primary ministry. Whether or not they are victims of poverty, they all need love, and Pat and I have much to give. Helping is a joyful privilege.

In 1966, one year after opening the Evangelical Home for Boys, we discovered Psalm 115:14: "May the Lord make you increase, both you and your children." We took this person-ally as a message from God, who would bless our work and make us positive examples to our boys. Perhaps the verse also promised us children of our own.

We wanted children. I suppose most couples do, but in our culture they are particularly important. For that reason I felt Patricia's frustration when she didn't immediately get preg-nant. My inquisitive family and neighbors meant only to show interest, of course, but to her their concern seemed meddlesome.

Eventually, on June 12, 1968, Patricia gave birth to a delightful little girl. We named her Susan—"lily of the valley"—in honor of Bob and Susan Grupp (it is also a common Arab name). Four years later, May 25, 1972, we had another girl and named her Hilary, the name of my grandmother ("Farha" in Arabic). Our third daughter, Rosemary (an English name), was born on May 11, 1973.

As with other families, our children have brought both joy and sorrow. Susan completed the nine years offered by our Evangelical School and graduated three years later from the Lutheran School in Ramallah; she then followed in my footsteps and attended Aurora University in the United States, graduating with top honors in 1989. Hilary also attended the Evangelical School and then the Friends Girls' School in Ramallah, until the military closed it in 1988. She completed high school in England and enrolled at Aurora in the fall of 1989.

Hilary was a tiny baby when Patricia became pregnant with our third child, Rosemary. For some reason Pat felt that she should have the delivery in England. Although as a missionary she had delivered hundreds of babies and given birth to our two in Jerusalem, Pat had no preparation for Rosemary's birth. Rosemary was severely brain damaged—so much so that at first the doctors expected her to live only a few days.

Not educable, Rosemary would always be completely dependent. We faced a grim question: Should Patricia leave Rosemary behind when she returned to the Middle East? We wanted to care for our new baby, but understood what permanent full-time childcare would mean for Patricia. Also, medical facilities were better in England. Reluctantly, we accepted the doctors' advice. Rosemary now lives with Nick and Lorraine Fuller and their family in Kidderminster in the English Midlands.

Knowing firsthand the benefits of specialized private foster care, we still affirm our decision. It is ironic that although we devote our lives to dependent children, we cannot care for our own dependent child. Perhaps this increases our empathy for our boys' parents and makes us better foster parents.

And how rewarding our work has been! We provide a desperately needed service. Due to its history, the Middle East has fallen behind the West. Palestine languished for four hundred years as a distant outpost in the Ottoman Empire. Interestingly, the Ottomans gained control of Palestine in 1517, the same year Martin Luther sparked Europe's Protestant Reformation, and only a quarter century after Columbus sailed from Spain to the new world. Four centuries of isolation and neglect began for us at the same time the Western world started to advance with astounding speed in education and technology. The Ottomans and later the British, who came in 1917, never developed us technologically, except in ways that would directly benefit them. Their legacies left Palestine far behind much of the world in science, medicine, technology, and agriculture. The Jordanian and Israeli occupiers did little to help us catch up.

In other ways we are far ahead of Europe and the United States. Middle Eastern culture has much to teach the more ethnocentric, aggressive, acquisitive Westerners regarding human relationships. Most outsiders never comprehend our deep human concern. Nevertheless, Palestinians have enormous economic and social needs.

My own inadequacy calls me to my power source, the divine center of my life, Jesus Christ. I ponder his message on the Mount of Olives, just ten miles from my home. In Matthew 25:34–40, Jesus as coming King praises those he will reward in his kingdom:

> For I was hungry and you gave me something to eat, I was
> thirsty and you gave me something to drink, I was a stranger
> and you invited me in, I needed clothes and you clothed me. I
> was sick and you looked after me, I was in prison and you
> came to visit me.
> Then the righteous will answer him, "Lord, when did we see
> you hungry and feed you, or thirsty and give you something to
> drink? When did we see you a stranger and invite you in, or
> needing clothes and clothe you? When did we see you sick or
> in prison and go to visit you?
> The King will reply, "I tell you the truth, whatever you did
> for one of the least of these brothers of mine, you did for me.

We are inundated by hungry, thirsty, sick, imprisoned, and
unclothed brothers of Jesus. We try to be strength to their
weaknesses. Our boys come from homes with one or both
parents dead, or from families so large the children lack care.
Palestinians on the West Bank and Gaza Strip have no social
security, no unemployment insurance, no medical or life
insurance, and only a limited chance for good employment.
West Bank workers pay into Israel's social security system, but
receive no benefits. If the government returned in services all
that West Bank Palestinians pay in taxes, we would have few
social problems.

I know mothers of six or seven children who lost their
husbands to death, imprisonment, or deportation. They have
no public services and many lack adequate jobs. In other
instances both parents are at home, but unable to find
employment. Extended families try to provide assistance, but
often cannot do enough. Also, the military occupation since
1967 has forcibly separated many families, increasing child
dependency. We meet these needs when we can.

Since 1988 the military government has usually kept all
Palestinian schools closed, elementary through university.
Although underground education continues, the denial of

formal schooling multiplies our social problems. Although our Evangelical School has been closed most of that time, we provide as much informal education as possible.

Patricia and I are only two of many trying to bridge the gap. Many service agencies, some of them the result of Christian missions, have inspired me over the years. One example is the Mennonite Central Committee, an American-based group that came here after 1948 to provide relief for refugees. Their impressive projects include needlework cooperatives, support for farmers, and water conservation. As early as 1952 they established a program in Hebron that eventually became the independently operated Arab Evangelical Orphanage, where they house and, when allowed, provide elementary education for over a hundred children.

Lutherans, Catholics, and other Christian groups also maintain significant projects, many offering health services, education, training, and agricultural assistance. The Quakers began their Friends Boys' and Friends Girls' schools in Ramallah over a century ago and, when the military government permits, still provide superior education. Many other academic and social projects grew from a spiritual concern for the Arabs. Each started as the missionary vision of Europeans or Americans, but all depend on a cooperative relationship with local Arab leaders who make the programs applicable to the grass roots.

I especially appreciate the homegrown projects; for example, the work of the Four Homes of Mercy in Bethany and Beit Jala impresses me. Concerned Arabs started and manage this outstanding service, which for a half-century has provided care for crippled and homeless children, as well as dependent, aged, and unwed mothers. In Ramallah several schools attempt to educate young people. One home serves the mentally retarded, another (in addition to our own) cares for dependent boys, and several other impressive projects attempt to solve particular physical and economic problems. The Palestinian people, although consistently short on funds, are long on merciful, loving concern for their fellow human beings.

A new outburst of social concern accompanied the intifada. After the Israelis closed our schools, local education committees formed; when the authorities closed shops, cut off food sources, and destroyed gardens, the people shared as much as possible. (For example, at the Home we had some stored food, so during the day I made lists of the most needy people and secretly distributed food to doorsteps at night.) When the iron fist left large numbers destitute, many doctors, nurses, and other professionals organized and offered free services.

Of all the service projects I have observed through the years, the Home of the Sons was the most important for me personally. It gave me a chance in life; I do not know where I would be today if it had not been for Carl Agerstrand and Robert Grupp. The second major influence was the Evangelical Home for Girls and the Evangelical School, started by Mary Jeanne Grupp, Keturah Morgan, and Gladys Thomas. As missionaries sacrificing for my people, these leaders exemplified the heart of Christ's kingdom. They influenced me to devote my life to children.

These projects, organized to help the refugees of 1948, inspired me to return to Ramallah in 1965. Since opening the Evangelical Home for Boys, we have housed more than two hundred dependent children, some for just a few months, others for more than fifteen years. We provide food, shelter, security, love, and a knowledge of the Savior, Jesus Christ. Our boys provide mostly pleasant memories.

Our first boys beyond the original twelve were brothers from Jordan named Samir and Victor, ages two and five. They came to us in 1966 after their mother died when a discarded grenade exploded. Samir often toddled to our bed at night and appealed to "Ma, Ma," persuading Pat to let him in bed with us. Later we wanted to adopt him, but the government denied permission because he had not been in the West Bank on June 5, 1967, the date of the Israeli occupation. (Samir had gone back to Amman for summer recess two days earlier, so the authorities prohibited him from entering the West Bank except by special permit. Ten years later the military government stopped granting us permits to bring any boys at all from Jordan. Even those who were home for the summer could not return.) Today Samir lives in Amman and works in a farm equipment store. I see him occasionally. Victor has moved to Sweden.

Elias provides another of our many fond memories. His mother was a Jewish Christian from central Europe, his father an Arab. After several years with us, the Israeli army inducted him because his mother's status made him a Jew. He has kept in touch with us, and recently called from Lebanon. I hope the government never sends him to patrol Ramallah or the rest of the West Bank, because he would refuse. He says that he is a Palestinian and could never bear arms against his own people.

Despite many changes in membership, our large household remains a close-knit community with each individual sharing mutual concerns. Patricia revealed some insights into our family life in our newsletter of Christmas 1978. Generally, what she said then is still true today:

> What makes up the lives of our little boys? The elementary necessities of eating, sleeping, and learning to live together semi-close, studying, playing, and praying for others; plus the many extras—hiking, picnicking, and amateur football

matches, television, singing songs, and monthly birthday parties.

During the first three years we lived in a very small house (three bedrooms—Patricia and I in one, six boys in each of the others). From 1968 to 1970 we occupied a larger, but still inadequate building. We rejoiced when, after five years of marriage, it became possible to rent four adjacent flats, which became a home large enough for the four of us and our thirty-six boys. That house even had central heating!

We settled quickly and happily into our new house, but later the landlord attempted to evict us. He claimed that we had violated the contract by making it an institution and by holding religious services. We finally won the case after three wearying years in court. (Arab-operated local courts adjudicate domestic issues. Military courts try all cases involving "security.")

The landlord avoided me as much as possible while our case was pending. However, I wanted his friendship, and always offered smiles and greetings. He apologized later and we reconciled. This supports one of my heartfelt principles: If we treat others as they treat us, we lose our testimony.

While the case was in court, the landlord's son broke into our house. They caught, convicted, and jailed him, but I appealed and got him released. I believe Christians should not be vindictive.

The problem with the landlord reveals the advantage of owning one's own property. As early as 1974 we noted in our newsletter that "the only way we are going to establish a boys' home is to have our own building like the girls' home." Pointing out that we hoped to find land, we added: "To build a boys' home in these days of high costs seems a ridiculous mountain, but we praise God we are not trusting in the riches of a millionaire, but in the promise of a Father whose riches are inexhaustible."

So we began to hope, to dream, to plan. Gradually we transferred the vision to paper and by 1978 we secured land with the help of a gift from Oxfam in England. Khalil Nasir and Saleemeh Budran, two members of our local St. Andrew's Episcopal Church, sold it to us at a very reasonable price.

That year Reverend Herbert McComus arranged to send thirty-four members of Teen Missions, based in Miami Springs, Florida, came to help prepare the land; they broke ground and put up a retaining wall. The next year two teams of volunteer workers—from Teen Missions and Mission Outreach—arrived from the United States and did carpentry, painting, window framing, tuck-pointing, and other tasks. The Missions Outreach group joined us again in 1985, using their summer vacations to construct outside walls. With their help and that of others, we completed the roofing in 1986. Patricia expressed our feelings in the newsletter a year later:

> We praise God for all these willing workers and for their happy, loving spirit. We have lost count of the many volunteers who have worked on the building. Both groups and individuals have helped by mixing cement, carrying buckets of gravel, painting window bars, laying electricity cables and whitewashing ceilings. Our boys have helped a lot, too, and some "old" boys have visited and joined in.

We appreciate the volunteers' service as servants of the Lord. To maximize the benefit to us, most even provide money for their own food and help us to prepare it.

John Woodger, rector of St. Mary's Church in Watford, England, provides a sparkling example. He brought one group for a work trip, and has helped us in many ways through the years. Most important is his friendship and support; he is sensitive to our needs. A close friend and dear brother, John understands the problems the Palestinians face, and responds accordingly.

Other interested friends provide financial gifts. For example, John and Kathleen Halstead gave us £9,000 sterling.

However, we have suffered some disappointments. One organization encouraged us to apply for a large grant. We spent many days visiting architects and contractors, getting estimates, and filling out forms. After waiting a long time, we received a letter saying that funding had decreased and they could not help us.

Several organizations have helped us make reduced cost purchases of furniture and other needed items. For example, in 1987 the Mennonite Central Committee found a good price on dining room tables and library chairs in the United States, and also provided reasonable delivery. A year later I went to the United States and ordered library shelves to be delivered in one of the MCC shipments.

We continue to depend on God for our daily needs. Nothing really has changed since in Swansea I trusted God for items as insignificant as a stamp and a bus ticket. He always provides, or shows us that we can get by without it. He gave his life to save us and gives us a new life; compared to that, material needs fade into insignificance. As we learn to depend on him for physical necessities, we learn to value the spiritual. If we worry about our daily bread, we show our failure to trust. So we look to him and let him teach us and make us effective servants, thereby proving that he answers prayer and cares for his own.

Occasionally, he provides in a dramatic way. One evening Pat told me of a telephone call asking that I go to Jerusalem and meet an American tourist who wanted to see me. I did not know who had given him my name, or why he wanted me, but I felt I should go. It took a while to find him, but when I did he handed me some money, and announced: "Please accept this in the name of the Lord." Upon opening the envelope I found exactly the amount we needed to pay several overdue bills.

Late in 1988 we moved into one floor of our new building. What a memorable day! At that point we could anticipate the culmination of our dream. By 1990 we had completed the kitchen, library, dining, and vocational training rooms. We had also prepared a medical clinic, to serve 3,000 people, and looked toward competion of the gymnasium room.

April 24, 1990, was a great day. In a joyous ceremony we dedicated the new Evangelical Home for Boys' facilities for the service of God and Palestinian youth.

I have performed various other ministries in addition to acting as father to a houseful of children, construction overseer, former deputy and acting mayor, and speaker to many visitors from America and Europe. Some deserve mention.

For several years I served as principal of the Evangelical School. The school, started by the women who ran the Evangelical Home for Girls, serves our children and many others in Ramallah. The enrollment runs about four hundred in kindergarten through ninth grade; more than one hundred live in our boys' and girls' homes. Since the intensification of the iron fist policy in 1988, however, the school has usually been closed.

I became assistant pastor of the Anglican Church in Ramallah in 1966. Ordained as deacon in 1968 and priest the following year, I have worked as a Christian minister in various capacities, including as rector of the Arabic congregation at St. George's Anglican Church in Jerusalem (preaching and doing pastoral visitation) and diocesan secretary for a year. For a time I conducted Sunday services in Ramallah, nearby Bir Zeit, and Haifa, about ninety miles away. I also preached in Gaza, about seventy miles distant.

In 1975, a longtime missionary to Egypt, Florence Christie, influenced the David C. Cook Publishing Company to have me translate Scripture from English to Arabic for a children's picture book. I wrote the New Testament message in simple-language picture captions. I also wrote Sunday school lessons on the reverse side of pictures (taking students through the entire Bible in six years), and helped in recording the words for a proposed hymnbook for the blind. Most of these late-night projects have been well worth the effort; some are widely used among Arabic-speaking Christians.

Since helping to start the Bethlehem Bible College in 1981, I have served on its board. When allowed to operate, the college trains young Palestinians in much the same way the Bible College of Wales trained me. It allows my people to learn to be teachers, preachers, or substitute parents in this country without training in a foreign land. This gives them immediate hands-on experience. It also alleviates the problem of so many never returning after going to school in another country.

Remembering that frightened eleven-year-old struggling toward Ramallah in 1948, I marvel at God's ability to use even the least of us. He can take the worst circumstances— the results of human greed and inhumanity—and produce good results. Who would have thought that in spite of the circumstances, I would go to school, find Patricia as my partner, and experience a joy-filled life of helping young people with backgrounds similar to my own?

Patricia and I desire to serve acceptably, praying that Jesus may become incarnate through what we say and do. Occasionally the problems almost overwhelm us. Our 1983 newsletter expressed some of our frustration, or perhaps our self-doubt:

> Sometimes we have wondered, is it worth it all? Are we putting stone upon stone in order to house and care for deprived children? Or are we building up young lives in the knowledge and love of Jesus Christ? At times when we are tempted to be discouraged we have had messages of appreciation and greeting from some of our "old boys." A letter from Amman, Jordan; an early morning telephone call from New York; a visit from one of the original twelve, about to get married; and one "old boy" even gave up his week's holiday from work to help us build. These tokens make it all worthwhile.

Sometimes the boys disappoint us and rebel against Christ. Sometimes we experience a deep sense of revival, with Jesus' presence filling their lives. In either case we pray that the teaching we give our boys will never leave them, and will neutralize their impulse to follow the evil, selfish ways of the world.

Sometimes I get frustrated and angry. I constantly knock my head against a bureaucratic wall, asking permission for this and that. The authorities always tell me to come tomorrow, and then tomorrow, and tomorrow ... It's maddening.

For example: Our daughter Susan graduated from Aurora University in 1989. Since as a West Bank Palestinian I have no country and no passport, my travel is at the whim of the military authorities. I repeatedly sought permission to attend her graduation, but the military government refused. Fortunately, Pat has an English passport, so she and her mother (from England) could attend.

Other intimidation continues. Although on January 10, 1990, military authorities reopened the school after nearly a year's closure, they arrested one of our boys and imprisoned one who formerly lived in the Home. In addition, they curfewed Ramallah the next month.

Later in 1990, Jews from a settlement two miles away entered the Evangelical School compound, threw rocks, and broke seventeen windows. As far as we know, they had no provocation except spite.

Several times in 1990, soldiers arrested our boys. For example, they held one twelve-year-old several hours, saying that he had thrown a stone at soldiers in downtown Ramallah. We feel sure he did not do it, but my assistant Todd Hicks, girls' home director Sister Vreni Wittwer, and I invested many hours in getting him released. It was maddening to hear the colonel charge that "all Arab boys throw stones" and "all Arab boys are liars."

As Father Louis Fevro of the Ramallah Roman Catholic Church prepared for Mass on February 11, 1990, he heard his congregation screaming, "Army, army!" Two soldiers, guns pointed, had chased some girls into the church. I asked Father Fevro to tell the story:

> I proceeded toward the altar when one of the soldiers began to click his machine gun, getting it ready to use. The soldier said the girls had been throwing stones at them.
>
> At that moment I raised my voice at the soldiers, saying: "Get out, get out. It is forbidden to enter holy places." I repeated for about ten times, "Get out," and after a fierce argument I succeeded in driving the two soldiers outside the church door. The entire congregation was extremely disturbed. Then one of the soldiers pointed his gun at me and said, "I am going to kill you." The other soldier hurriedly ran toward his colleague and stopped him. I then went to the altar to proceed with the Mass. The entire congregation was in a state of fear and shock.
>
> The soldiers stayed outside the church at the main gate by the main street. After the Mass was over and the congregation was leaving, the soldiers stopped the people and collected their

identity cards and made them wait until 12:00 noon, knowing that the Mass ended at 11:00 A.M.

We have learned to accept the bad with the good, and to praise the Lord anyway. Pat accurately summarized our nostalgia, and our hopes and dreams, in the newsletter of September 1980:

> How well I remember that first day—Sept. 1st, 1965, when twelve little Arab boys entered our home and shared our newly married life. Since that time 110 boys have passed through our home. . . . Some have responded to the Gospel and have kept in touch with us after leaving, continuing in the Christian faith; others we have lost touch with. Many emigrated to the USA, this being the pattern for so many Palestinian families, especially those with sons, because of the increasing pressures and insecurities of occupation and seeing a brighter future in the "new world."
>
> Through all these past fifteen years, we can say: "To God be the Glory, Great is thy Faithfulness." He continues to supply all our needs, and more.

We sent that letter many years ago, but our faith and our attitudes have not changed. We still resolve to share our faith, meet our neighbor's needs for shelter and love, and influence the world toward national freedom and justice.

We recently received a letter from a young man the Israelis have imprisoned. We hope his attitude is typical of the boys we have influenced:

> To my father Pastor Audeh Rantisi, I send you my warmest regards and say that the Lord is with us and He answers our prayers that come from the heart and in faith in Him our Lord and Saviour Jesus Christ.
>
> I send my heartiest greetings to my mother, Auntie Pat and Uncle Todd Hicks. I am always proud of the upbringing the Evangelical Home gave me. Greetings to all at the Home. I shall never forget the time I lived with all of you as one family faithful and true. Our Lord taught us to love our enemies and

to bless those who curse us. Forgive and you shall be forgiven. And our Lord, when He was on the cross said, "Father, forgive them for they don't know what they are doing."

We pray that we ourselves may live up to the training we gave this young man. Our goal is to be what our Lord requests of us. We want to be religious according to James' teaching: "Religion that God our Father accepts as pure and faultless is this: to look after orphans and widows in their distress and to keep oneself from being polluted by the world" (James 1:27).

We ask God to baptize us into this pure and faultless religion. May we seek no other goal.

APPENDIX

Many foreigners who visit the Evangelical Home for Boys want a Christian Palestinian's perspective on the issues here. I will answer some of the most common questions; however, I will not try to develop definitive answers to the complex problems of the Middle East. I will merely give one man's opinion about how we might approach the questions.

Question 1: What are your suggestions about how to solve the Palestinian problem?

By "the Palestinian problem" people mean the deep division between Israel and the Palestinians. First, I must say that I do believe a solution is possible, although the issues are difficult and people often intransigent. The solution rests on a willingness to compromise.

The controversy boils down to one simple fact: Two groups believe they have a justified claim to the same land. From this come many of the dilemmas in the Middle East, certainly most of those referred to by the term "Palestinian problem." Israel claims the biblical promise to Abraham (beginning in Genesis 12) and the right to return to ancestrally occupied lands. Palestinians want the right to live freely and with their own chosen government in the land occupied by family ancestors for hundreds of years.

First we must shatter all myths about getting everything we want. Neither side can have all of Palestine. Israel cannot have permanent military occupation of the West Bank and Gaza

Strip. Palestinians evicted in 1948 cannot have their homes back. The only reasonable solution requires two independent nations—Israel and Palestine—living side by side in the land between the Mediterranean Sea and the Jordan River, each with secure borders, each respecting the independence and rights of the other, each with enough land and water to live in dignity.

Many Israelis and their supporters have wanted a "for Jews only" state over all of Palestine, with all Palestinians driven across the river into Jordan. This solution is no more reasonable than forced eviction to Canada of everyone in the United States if Mexico wanted to expand northward. Others recommend that Israel annex the occupied territories. Some Palestinians accept this, but most Jews reject it, recognizing that demography dictates that within a few years Moslem and Christian Palestinians would outnumber Jews.

The crux of the problem is Palestinian representation: Who speaks for us? Every discussion of the controversy falters on this point. Virtually all Palestinians recognize the Palestine Liberation Organization as their government in exile and legitimate political representative. If Palestinians had the opportunity to choose, I am confident that well over 90 percent—probably 99 percent since the intifada—would endorse the PLO (although they would not totally agree about the various PLO factions).

Yet Israel and the United States want to negotiate the future of Palestine with Egypt, or Jordan, or Syria, but not with Palestine's own chosen representatives. For example, in the summer of 1989, the Likud government developed an "election" plan to precede negotiations—yet they proposed that they would decide which Palestinian candidates could run.

They excuse this behavior by referring to the PLO as a "terrorist organization." However, it commits no more violence than the governments of Israel, the United States, or Great Britain. If we were a nation with a recognized government, people would not use the term "terrorist" to describe our actions. World opinion judges violence committed by sovereign governments on the merits of the particular situation. As with other peace-loving nations, Palestine's government would defend its people against invasions, but would be no more violent than other independent nations.

Israel properly exercises the right to its own freely chosen government; Palestine should not meddle in its affairs. Equally, Palestine has the right to its own land and government; Israel should not maintain a military government over its land and people.

A comprehensive settlement of the Palestinian conflict requires recognizing the concerns and interests of both parties. Human and political rights cannot be fulfilled at the expense of either the Jewish or Palestinian peoples. For the sake of both the Jews and the Palestinians, we must break the vicious cycle of victims becoming oppressors.

These objectives require Israel to guarantee Palestine's right to exist as an independent nation, and Palestine to guarantee Israel's right to exist as an independent nation. The assurances must be so strong that people can never again say that Palestinians want to drive the Israelis into the sea, nor that the Israelis want to drive the Palestinians into the desert (Jordan, Lebanon, etc.).

United Nations Security Council Resolutions 242 and 338 provide the basis for a peaceful settlement, but only with the addition of a clear recognition that Palestine will become a sovereign nation, free to speak for itself in all negotiations. The principles in these resolutions must insure the withdrawal of troops and settlements from all territories occupied in 1967, and provide for all states in the area to live in peace with secure and recognized borders.

A solution requires long, difficult negotiations among Israel, a freely chosen Palestinian government, and other concerned nations. A transition team (presumably from the United Nations) would oversee the withdrawal of Israeli forces, evacuation of settlements, release of political prisoners, and the mechanics for establishing a constitution and democratic elections in Palestine. Logically, East and West Jerusalem would be the capitals, with all faiths guaranteed completely free, unrestricted access to the holy places. However, details must remain subject to negotiation.

A just peace requires significant concessions—but nations will do what they believe is in their own self-interest. Israeli self-interest demands these compromises, because today's hostility diminishes Israel. We can have peace with justice only if both sides relinquish that which has made peace and justice unavailable. An old Arab proverb asserts: "There is no problem without a solution; there is no climbing without a descent." Finding the solution to this problem requires a tough climb, a willingness to work at it, and a mutual respect for the humanness of the other party.

From self-respect and mutual respect will follow freedom from paranoia—a prerequisite for a secure peace. Security for Palestine depends on Israel's enjoying peace with justice; security for Israel depends on Palestine's enjoying peace with justice.

For many this transition requires a change in thought and in action. The result: two free, independent nations side by side, first living in tension with tightly patrolled borders, then gradually in trust.

Thousands of Jews and Arabs now speak out for moderation and the conciliation necessary to provide a better life for both peoples. Millions around the world share their concerns.

Although writing to those of all faiths, I especially appeal to fellow Christians to evenhandedly support peace with justice in the Holy Land.

"Blessed are the peacemakers, for they will be called sons of God" (Matt. 5:9).

Question 2: Is it realistic to think the problems can be solved without a bloody revolution?

John Kennedy served as President when I studied in the United States. He warned: "If we make nonviolent change impossible, we make violent change inevitable." Although speaking of Latin America, his message is true for the Holy Land.

Change is inevitable. Victimized in 1948 and 1967, West Bank and Gaza Strip residents cannot continue the post-1967 status quo. Signs of change appear for all who are willing to see. In the intifada the Palestinian people sound a clear call for freedom. There is no turning back.

I believe that if Palestinians had to choose between subjugation and death, most would choose death. This seems extreme, but a "liberty or death" ultimatum should not surprise Americans who know about Patrick Henry and their own revolution.

Must the road to freedom turn blood red? Rather, how can we find nonviolent solutions? For the answer, we look first to the Israelis and their supporters, since they have the power to effect immediate change. If they relinquish control of the occupied territories and give first-class citizenship to Palestinians living in Israel, they will have opted for nonviolence. If they continue to deter liberty and justice, they open the door to violence. Regrettably, the latter course has more historical precedent, since few controlling nations seem capable of accepting the realities until it is too late to prevent a bloodbath.

Nevertheless, Israel should have the capacity to transcend the behavior of traditional ruling powers. Until my generation, Jewishness symbolized a liberal concern for human rights. Sufferers of intense discrimination, Jews have always led the fight for civil liberties. Now paying a heavy price for the extremes of Zionism, the international Jewish community evinces frustration and embarrassment. The differences between the early utopian dream and the current ultra-conservative, liberty-denying nation begin to sensitize Jewish consciences and activate Jewish voices around the world.

I have heard some of these voices. Many of my Jewish friends fear that the iron-fist policy will lead to extensive bloodshed. Anxious to find a just solution and unwilling to see everything through myopic, expansionist eyes, they look to their liberal roots. Never comfortable as a military occupying power, many now agonize about rifles vs. rocks. They recognize that guns leveled on women and children maim the ones pulling the trigger.

Sadly, however, Israel so far seems no wiser than other authoritarian powers that have provoked revolutions. The government and its conservative supporters appear willing to risk everything for a military policy that in fact increases insecurity by gradually pushing Palestinians toward a violent response to violent action.

In 1988 the Israeli government exhibited convoluted thinking when it deported my friend Mubarak Awad (brother of Bishara Awad, who runs the Bethlehem Bible College, and husband of Nancy Nye, former principal of the Friends Girls' School). Mubarak is a Palestinian Christian who, modeling Jesus Christ's call for peace as a way of life, initiated the Center for the Study of Non-Violence. The government's pretense was that Mubarak, although Jerusalem-born and a resident here most of his life, also became a United States' citizen. In rejecting nonviolent, moderate spokespersons for change, the government leaves violence as the only recourse. Yet mimicking Israel's militancy would only diminish ourselves and our cause. One cannot use the methods of the oppressor without also becoming tainted.

Palestinians must find the courage to emulate the many who advocate nonviolent direct action. We may not produce a Mahatma Gandhi or a Martin Luther King, Jr., but we can unitedly engage in tactics similar to these magnificent men of India and America. Thereby we can claim the moral stature available only to those who refuse to dehumanize the adversary.

"We shall overcome some day!" was the chorus black Americans repeated when I was in the United States. Through the years they have progressed significantly. Yet to overcome does not imply grinding the Jewish adversary into the ground, any more than overcoming meant to establish black rule over white. Palestinians can find true freedom only by respecting the humanness of the Jews and seeing them as God's children. We must reject the temptation to sink to vindictiveness. Always we must acknowledge our adversary's dignity.

Since Israeli viciousness is a function of insecurity, Palestinians need to proclaim that freedom and justice for us will bring security to them. They must understand that our independence will enhance their dreams.

We will gain independence some day. Already Palestinians have the unity that resulted from years of resistance and culminated in the intifada. It is not outer, but inner strength, a belief in oneself, a determination to gain the respect that comes with human rights. In the intifada we face weapons without retreat. Our people are mostly nonviolent—and by maintaining that stance, we will win the consciences of a concerned world. Our revolution will succeed when world opinion turns against the oppressor. World opinion will turn to us as we refuse to dehumanize the Jews by hating and shooting them. As Martin Luther King proclaimed, "Unearned suffering is redemptive."

We in the Middle East have a cultural predilection for community problem-solving. Some Palestinian villages still practice the *sulha,* the ancient Arab method of bringing antagonists together. When a dispute or a blood feud occurs, village elders appeal to both parties, sometimes returning repeatedly—ten, twenty, thirty times—eventually making resolution possible. The offended and the offender meet before the entire community and vow reconciliation and forgiveness. Then the community shares a celebration feast. To break the vow brings shame. In many instances the *sulha* can be better than adversary court procedures, which often bring enmity and division. The procedure is infinitely better than bloodshed.

This suggests that to some degree, at least, Palestinians may have more affinity for nonviolence than the more materialistic, militant Zionists, who reflect the individualistic Western cultures. Rooted in the family-oriented, community-minded Middle East, Palestinian traditions may provide a mindset that more easily leads to patient, unselfish solutions to problems.

I quoted from Raja Shehadeh in chapter 9 of this book. Raja calls for a third way, "between mute submission and blind hate." He quotes his Jewish friend, Enoch:

> After so much suffering, killing, distrust—there need to be some rituals of truce, of mutual confessions of wrongdoing, so that a more genuine intimacy may grow on the seedbed of despair. In short, we must beg each other's forgiveness, and if people cannot come in their pride to humble themselves before one another, then perhaps we can all, in our own way but together, ask forgiveness of a higher power.

Shehadeh continues:

> Like many Palestinians, I used to see it as inevitable that the survivors of the holocaust would be driven by such hate and fear that they would act ruthlessly to ensure their own preservation, regardless of who paid for it. But Enoch remembers the evil perpetrated against his people, remembers it deeply, without himself being a hate-blinded, vengeance-seeking victim of that wrong. In him I see that really honouring the memory of people who have suffered creates courage and a capacity for love that cannot be equalled by someone who does not remember or acknowledge man's capacity for evil. What I have learned from Enoch has made me expect more from the Jews—which is not easy because it opens a place for hope and its betrayal. But even more important, it has taught me to expect more of myself—never to excuse in myself the psychology of a victim—someone whose actions and reactions you can understand, in the circumstances, but not respect.[1]

In conclusion, the key questions are these: Can we somehow prevent the bloody revolutionary war that almost seems inevitable? Will Israel allow change without being forced into it? If not, will the Palestinians be creative enough to shake off the occupation without major violence?

We can avoid the tragedy of war. War allows no winner, only misery, destruction, vindictiveness, and revenge on both sides. Dogmatic self-righteousness already abounds in the Holy Land. Another war would make it worse, resulting in long-continued animosity and severely diminished hope that the two nations might ever live peacefully in the land between the Mediterranean and the Jordan.

I pray that Israel will understand this and help us. She has so much to lose by refusing to reject her obsession with control. In the eyes of mankind the sword-wielding Goliath will fall. And when we win the moral battle for world opinion, we win the victory.

We need help from those who can support us. We do not need their guns. We do need their prayers, their active, concerned consciences, and their influence on those who have power but lack the will to treat Israelis and Palestinians equally. Israel also needs help, perhaps more than we, because whenever the iron fist policy costs the Jews their posture as victims of unearned suffering, they squander the moral ascendancy that has made their nation unique. Then they expose themselves as just another self-seeking imperialistic nation, and the doors again open to the anti-Semitism that is the blight of European history. There are limits to power. By its military occupation, Israel has exceeded those limits.

Outside nations, particularly the United States, should save the Jews from the Zionist impulse to control more and more land. In doing so they may save the Palestinians from taking up the sword. If the United States would be evenhanded and helpful to both sides, it could no longer claim Israel as its only friend in the Middle East. Palestine would also be a friend, as would much of the Arab world.

I turn to the Holy Bible, my source of inspiration and conviction. The apostle Paul echoed Jesus when he wrote:

> Do not repay anyone evil for evil. . . . If it is possible, as far as it depends on you, live at peace with everyone. Do not take revenge, my friends, but leave room for God's wrath, for it is written: "It is mine to avenge; I will repay," says the Lord. On the contrary: "If your enemy is hungry, feed him; if he is thirsty, give him something to drink. . . ." Do not be overcome by evil, but overcome evil with good (Rom. 12:17–21).

Question 3: God commanded Joshua to take over this land and destroy the Canaanites. Why should you resist His command to the Zionists to do the same thing?

I find unthinkable any comparison of the irreligious twentieth-century Zionists with Joshua, who accepted God's commandment to "be careful to obey all the law . . ." (Josh. 1:7). God's promises to the children of Israel require obedience, while most Zionists pay little attention to God. God completed his promises in Jesus and his spiritual descendants, not in any body of land.

God delivered Israel from Egypt to develop a faithful nation, one he could use. He covenanted in Deuteronomy 29 and 30 that the children of Israel must "obey the Lord your God and keep his commands and decrees that are written in the Book of the Law and turn to the Lord your God with all your heart and with all your soul" (Deut. 30:10).

If they disobeyed? "You will not live long in the land you are crossing the Jordan to enter and possess" (Deut. 30:18). Then he put it to them directly: "I have set before you life and death, blessings and curses. Now choose life, so that you and your children may live and that you may love the Lord your God, listen to his voice, and hold fast to him" (vv. 19–20).

Joshua himself proclaimed that he and his household would serve the Lord. When the Israelites agreed to "serve the Lord our God and obey him" (Josh. 24:24), Joshua warned of God's punishment if they reneged. Then he made a covenant containing laws for the people, set a stone under an oak tree at Shechem (Nablus), and announced: "This stone will be a witness . . . against you if you are untrue to your God" (v. 27).

Sometimes the children of Israel obeyed and prospered; often they disobeyed and God punished. Judges and the books of Samuel and the Chronicles report a hard history, with unbelief and disobedience causing eventual dispersion.

Once, when allowed to return from exile and rebuild Jerusalem's city wall, Nehemiah discovered in the temple ruins the Book of the Law. Upon reading it, he echoed Joshua in calling the people to repentance for their sins and those of their forefathers. Put away your idols and return again to the house of God, he insisted. As with Joshua, obedience was the key to God's favor.

God wanted them to remember that their military prowess did not bring the victories. He had cleared the land for them: "I gave them into your hands. I sent the hornet ahead of you. . . . You did not do it with your own sword and bow" (Josh. 24:11–12). The "conquest" was merely an act of God, conditioned on Israel's obedience.

Twentieth-century Zionists have little of Joshua's faith and godliness. Most are atheists or agnostics who pay no attention to God's commandments. By using the "chosen nation" image to justify their land-hungry aggression, they attempt to convince the Judeo-Christian world to support actions Joshua would have condemned: "He is a holy God," proclaimed the great Old Testament leader. "He will not forgive your rebellion and your sins. If you forsake the Lord and serve foreign gods, he will turn and bring disaster on you and make an end of you" (Josh. 24:19–20).

Although many of the Old Testament prophets were addressing ancient Israel, they could have been speaking today when they predicted God would "punish Israel for her sins," and allow an enemy to overrun the land (Amos 3:11, 14). The antidote? "Let justice roll on like a river, righteousness like a never-failing stream!" (Amos 5:24). And "What does the Lord require of you? To act justly and to love mercy and to walk humbly with your God" (Micah 6:8). God linked the call to obedience with a requirement that Israel promote justice.

God may not choose to wreak immediate vengeance upon disobedient, unjust twentieth-century Israel. Yet God's punishment of the disobedient Old Testament Israelites suggests that nations supporting rebellious Israel today may be in peril.

I understand why the irreligious Zionists use religion as a convenient and effective aid to their political goals. Nations have used this ploy throughout history. Israel mirrors many governments in successfully linking the Judeo-Christian religious heritage to its own political goals.

More difficult to comprehend, however, is the unconditional support some Christians confer upon unchristlike Israel. They consider Jews, as God's chosen people, accountable to no moral or ethical standards; God blesses them no matter what they do. The world should applaud and support the Israelis, according to popular reasoning, even when they behave immorally. Christians should influence their governments to uphold Israel even when the Israelis obey neither the teachings of Jesus nor the laws of Old Testament Israel.

This stance seriously distorts Jesus' message and undermines Christian work in the Middle East. Our own evangelistic work in Ramallah suffers from these "Christian Zionists." Infatuated with secular Israel, they attempt to evangelize Jews only as a corollary to their resolute support of the nation's aggressive political and military goals.

Supporting those goals is antithetical to Christ's teaching. Ironically, today's Israel considers it better for Jews to be agnostic or atheist than Christian. Most Jews claim no belief in God, yet Israeli society accepts them completely; those who come to Jesus Christ and change their identity cards to "Christian," open themselves to social ostracism and severe discrimination.

Appendix

I know of about five thousand Hebrew-speaking Christians who have converted from Judaism. Their leader in Tel Aviv, Chaim Leibovitz, accepted Jesus in Jerusalem about fifty years ago. Since 1948 Israel has denounced him (and others like him) as a kind of political traitor. Today he and his compatriots pray that Christians throughout the world will soon display as much concern for Jewish Christians who do not support Israel's militaristic goals as for atheists who do. (Many converted Jews avoid much discrimination by maintaining the classification of "Jew" on their identity cards; the Hebrew-speaking Christians refuse to do this. In Israel, loyalty to the Jewish state is far more important than personal religious experience.)

My understanding of prophecy and the gospel message is very different from Christians who unreservedly support Israeli politics. The real Israel—the Israel of God—comprises Jews and Gentiles who have submitted their lives to Jesus Christ and his purposes. The truly significant call of God is to faith, not to a land. God created heaven and world—he owns it all. Christ came and died for the entire earth. Those who trust and believe on him—Jews and Gentiles alike—become children of Abraham by faith.

God has a plan in history. He created a marvelous world; Jesus died as an atonement for human sin and makes his truth available to whoever believes in him (John 3:16); in the end God will win the victory over Satan and the evil forces of this world.

God's plan included Joshua, but we cannot infer that disobedient Zionists are doing his work. The Israel of God includes all people who accept Jesus Christ and live in obedience to his will.

Question 4: What recommendations have you for foreigners wanting to promote Christianity in the Holy Land?

I love missionaries. Who knows where I would be today if it were not for Carl Agerstrand and Bob Grupp's mission work at the Home of the Sons in Ramallah? I went to a missions-oriented Bible college and served as a missionary in the Sudan. I married a missionary.

I give my blessing to anyone who feels God's call to preach the Word, the good news, and uplift those who suffer from economic or political deprivation. Service in God's kingdom is a high privilege; I delight in it.

Were the church to lose its zeal to spread God's message—that Jesus died for our salvation and to give us life and spiritual power—it would no longer be the church as he ordained it. He called his followers to witness in Jerusalem, the West Bank (at that time called Judea and Samaria), and "to the ends of the earth" (Acts 1:8). Very early some of the people of Palestine (including all who were in Lydda) became Christians as a result of this calling.

Today some Christians reverse the Great Commission and come from the ends of the earth to witness in the West Bank and Jerusalem. Some do much good and bring a blessing; others seem motivated principally by the desire for their church to have a presence in the Holy Land. Some express interest only in the Jews, seeing them as more important spiritually than other human beings. Ironically, these Christians identify more closely with secular, nonpracticing Jews than with either Moslem or Christian Palestinians. Many give strong political support to the Zionists, condone anything Israel does, and damage the work of Jesus Christ among the Palestinians.

Others come to look at the rocks. I understand the fascination of this historical and archaeological gold mine. I share the excitement, and enjoy walking where Jesus and the patriarchs walked. However, many who study here seem interested only in the stones of civilizations past and ignore the living stones of the church today. I wish more foreign Christians sought today's reality along with yesterday's relics.

To be effective missionaries, foreigners need to ally themselves with the existing work here. They should come as servants to the local leaders, anxious to help, but not to dictate from the vantage point of Western culture. In our work in Ramallah we have found that nearly all those who assist us display sensitivity. They become good missionaries because, understanding that we know the local situation, they try to help us toward our own goals.

In summary, I applaud missionary efforts here and throughout the world. (Sometimes, though, it seems that Palestinian Christians should go as missionaries to western Europe and the United States to share a more Christlike gospel than seems the norm there.) Jesus Christ called us to witness everywhere to those who need his salvation. We all need to carry out his will, wherever we are.

Question 5: How can foreigners best help the Jews? How can they best help the Palestinians?

I put these two questions together because the answers are so similar. Respecting the integrity of both Palestinians and Israelis, outsiders can help them determine how they can solve their political problems. They can encourage both groups to work toward positive goals.

The interests of the two parties are parallel: *Israelis will never realize their dreams until Palestine is a secure nation; Palestinians will never realize their dreams until Israel is a secure nation.* I anticipate the day when both Semitic groups will be free to sit in contentment under their own vines and fig trees—a day when they will beat their swords into plowshares and their spears into pruning hooks, make the desert bloom, practice Middle Eastern hospitality, and enjoy peace together. Outsiders can help make this happen.

Nevertheless, I do not expect a utopia. There may always be tensions, and a perfect life will never come on this earth. Still, I note that Great Britain and France, who once fought constantly, have been friends for nearly two centuries. The United States and Germany fought two terrible twentieth-century wars, but now cooperate. For this to happen with Arabs and Jews, the outside world must offer significant assistance.

Every interested person should encourage his or her own government to deal evenhandedly with the two peoples and expedite a just peace. Concurrently, each person can pray and support Jewish and Palestinian organizations that work to promote a just peace.

For most foreigners this requires study. People generally display ignorance of this land's history and culture. Many come here with deep prejudices against Arabs in general and Palestinians in particular. Many have a deeply established pro-Israeli bias, often based on Christian concern but in ignorance of the real situation.

On the other hand I have discovered that many people sincerely want to learn the whole story. Each year several groups stop at the Evangelical Home for Boys and some ask perceptive questions, suggesting concern and eagerness to understand. This may have increased since the intifada and iron fist policy began. Many people show genuine concern. When they do, I am encouraged.

Through the prophet Amos, God gave his stern directive: "But let justice roll on like a river, righteousness like a never-failing stream!" (Amos 5:24). Quoting the old law, Jesus himself clearly made this point: 'Love the Lord your God

Appendix

with all your heart and with all your soul and with all your
strength and with all your mind' and 'Love your neighbor as
yourself' (Luke 10:27).

If foreigners could practice this commandment in their
relationships with us, they would help us immensely. Jews
and Palestinians alike would benefit. We welcome their
assistance.

CHRONOLOGY

c. 1900 B.C.	Abraham travels from Ur to Canaan
c. 1700 B.C.	Jacob's family settles in Egypt
c. 1300 B.C.	Joshua leads Israelites into Canaan
c. 1000 B.C.	David reigns as king of Israel
c. 930 B.C.	Israel divides into two kingdoms
c. 722 B.C.	Northern kingdom destroyed by Assyrians
c. 587 B.C.	Southern kingdom destroyed by Babylonians
c. 538 B.C.	Persians permit Jews to return to Jerusalem
332 B.C.	Greeks under Alexander conquer the region
167 B.C.	Jews revolt, establish independent Judea
63 B.C.	Romans win control of Palestine
4 B.C.	Jesus is born in Bethlehem
29 A.D.	Jesus crucified and resurrected
70+ A.D.	Jewish revolt suppressed, second temple destroyed, Romans take Masada. Many Jews exiled.
132+	Jews revolt and most are exiled
622+	Islam spreads over Palestine
1099	European crusaders take Jerusalem
1187	Moslems recapture Jerusalem
1517	Ottoman Turks take Jerusalem
1882	First European Zionists migrate to Holy Land
1897	First World Zionist Congress meets in Basel, Switzerland
1914–17	In return for support in war, Britain promises both Jews and Arabs future state on same land in Palestine
1922	League of Nations authorizes British mandate over Palestine and Transjordan

1932–46	Saudi Arabia, Egypt, Syria, Lebanon, Jordan become independent nations
1937	Audeh Rantisi born in Lydda, current site of Ben Gurion Airport
1947	United Nations partitions Palestine between immigrant Jews and native Palestinians
1948	State of Israel proclaimed. Nothing done to encourage Palestinian state. At least 700,000 Arabs lose their homes, become refugees. Israel tries to expand into territory U.N. has designated for Palestinians and threaten surrounding Arab nations. Arab nations try to destroy Israel. Rantisi family among those driven from Lydda to Ramallah.
1949	Arab-Israeli war ends. West Bank becomes part of Jordan and Gaza Strip becomes part of Egypt
1952	Audeh Rantisi acts on John 3:16, becomes Christian in personal sense
1955–58	Audeh Rantisi attends Bible College of Wales
1956	Egypt nationalizes Suez Canal. Israel invades Egypt
1960–63	Audeh Rantisi attends Aurora College (now University) in Illinois
1963–65	Audeh serves as missionary in Sudan
1965	Audeh marries Patricia Greening of Shrewsbury, England. They open Evangelical Home for Boys in Ramallah, West Bank
1967	In "Six Day War" Israel takes military control of West Bank and Gaza Strip. Israel ignores U.N.'s demand that it withdraw (Security Council Resolution 242)
1968	Susan Rantisi born on June 12
1972	Hilary Rantisi born on May 25
1973	Rosemary Rantisi born on May 11 "Yom Kipper" War

1974	Arabs at Rabat conference proclaim PLO as sole legitimate representative of the Palestinian people
1976	Audeh Rantisi elected Ramallah's deputy mayor in only free election Israel has allowed in the Occupied Territories
1977	Anwar Sadat visits Jerusalem
1978	Israel invades Lebanon in attempt to destroy PLO
	Jimmy Carter hosts Anwar Sadat and Menachim Begin at Camp David. Peace agreement signed, but Palestinians not represented, and no progress made toward establishment of Palestinian state
	Land purchased for permanent Evangelical Home for Boys
1982	Israel again invades Lebanon, seeking to destroy PLO
1983	Suicide bombing attack in Beirut kills 241 American marines
1987	Intifada begins in Occupied Territories
1988	Palestine declares independence on November 15.
	PLO leadership recognizes Israel's right to exist, but Israel still fails to recognize Palestine's right to exist
	One floor of permanent Evangelical Home for Boys occupied
1990	Evangelical Home for Boys dedicated on April 24

NOTES

chapter two

1. Wesley G. Pippert, *Land of Promise, Land of Strife: Israel at Forty* (Waco, Texas: Word Books, 1988), 128, and other sources.

2. David Hirst, *The Gun and the Olive Branch* (London: Faber and Faber, 1984), 85.

3. This familiar statement often has been attributed to Theodore Herzl, but probably originated earlier.

4. Balfour's letter to Lord Rothschild is quoted in its entirety in David Hirst, *The Gun and the Olive Branch* (London: Faber and Faber, 1984), 38, and many other sources.

5. Hirst, *The Gun and the Olive Branch*, 63.

6. Ibid., 63.

7. Hirst, *The Gun and the Olive Branch*, 93, quoting Walid Khalidi, *From Haven to Conquest*, 846–49 for the Arab figures and *The Times* (July 21, 1938); *A Survey of Palestine*, Jerusalem, 1946, 38–49 for the Jewish and British deaths. Hirst points out that, if translated into contemporary British or American terms, the Arab death figures for the three years would represent 200,000 British or 1,000,000 Americans killed.

8. A discussion of the 1939 White Paper in which this policy was announced is included in most works on this period, including Hirst, 95–96.

9. Menachem Begin, *In the Underground*, 21–25, quoted in Amos Perlmutter, *The Partitioned State* (New York: Charles Scribner's Sons, 1985), 101.

10. Hirst, *The Gun and the Olive Branch*, 38.

11. David K. Shipler, *Wounded Spirits in a Promised Land* (New York: Penguin Books, 1987), 32–33.

12. Shipler, *Wounded Spirits in a Promised Land*, 39.

13. Ibid., 37.

Notes

14. Menachem Begin, *The Revolt,* rev. ed. (New York: Nash Publishing, 1977), 164 ff.
15. Khalidi, 800; quoting "Jewish Newsletter," February 9, 1959.
16. Sami Hadawi, *Palestine: Loss of a Heritage* (San Antonio, Texas: The Naylor Company, 1963), 35–36.
17. Jon and David Kimche, *Both Sides of the Hill* (London: Secker and Warburg, 1960), 227–28.
18. Ethel Mannin, *The Road to Beersheba* (Chicago: Henry Regnery Company, 1963), 17–18.
19. David Neff, *Warriors For Jerusalem: The Six Days That Changed The Middle East* (New York: Linden Press/Simon & Schuster, 1984), 23–24.
20. Hirst, *The Gun and the Olive Branch,* 142–43.

chapter three

1. Mannin, *The Road to Beersheba,* 42–43.
2. Folke Bernadotte, *To Jerusalem* (London: Hodder and Stoughton, 1951), 200.
3. United Nations document, quoted in Sami Hadawi, *Palestine: Loss of a Heritage* (San Antonio, Texas: The Naylor Company, 1963), 40–41.
4. In *This Year in Jerusalem* (London: Darton, Longman & Todd, 1982), 30, Kenneth Cragg suggests that the Stern Gang assassinated Bernadotte because, although his work had materially helped Israel's cause, he was too conciliatory: "He collided with the momentum in the Israeli mood." "Had he succeeded," Cragg argues, "the future would have been different—and peaceful."
5. Amos Perlmutter, *The Partitioned State* (New York: Charles Scribner's Sons, 1985), 124.
6. Naim Nassar is now the Lutheran bishop in Jerusalem and Elias Asi is a pastor in the Church of the Nazarene in the United States.

chapter four

1. Martin Luther King, Jr., *Strength to Love* (Philadelphia: Fortress Press, 1963, 1982), 51–53.

chapter six

1. Moshe Dayan, *Diary of the Sinai Campaign* (London: Weidenfield and Nicholson, 1966), 21.

chapter seven

1. Russell Watson with Milan J. Kubic, "Israel Wages Economic War," *Newsweek* (March 28, 1988), 40.
2. Quoted in Geoffrey Aronson, *Creating Facts: Israel, Palestinians and the West Bank* (Washington, D.C.: Institute for Palestinian Studies, 1987), 267. (By "Judea and Samaria" Shamir meant the West Bank, using the biblical terms that had become the official Israeli name for the West Bank.)
3. Aronson, *Creating Facts,* 268.
4. Quoted in Aronson, *Creating Facts,* 5, 302.

chapter eight

1. *Al-Fajr*, September 14–20, 1980, 3.
2. Perlmutter, *The Partitioned State,* 314.
3. Ibid., 311.

chapter nine

1. Amnesty International USA, "Town Arrest Orders in Israel and the Occupied Territories," October 2, 1984, 35.
2. Russell, "Israel Wages Economic War," 40.
3. Yehoshafat Harkabi, quoted in Friend Committee on National Legislation, *Washington Newsletter*, June 1988, 1.
4. *Los Angeles Times,* April 12, 1988.
5. Michael Lerner, "The Occupation: Immoral and Stupid," *Tikkun,* Vol. 3, No. 2, n.d. reprint.
6. Lerner, "The Occupation: Immoral and Stupid," 3.
7. Minister of State David Mellor, upon visit to Jabaliya camp in Gaza Strip, as quoted in *Boston Globe* (January 5, 1988).
8. "Amnesty Action," published by the United States Section of Amnesty International, March/April, 1988.
9. Raja Shehadeh, *The Third Way, A Journal of Life in the West Bank* (London: Quartet Books, 1982), 141.
10. Mubarak Awad is married to Nancy Nye, former principal of the Friends Girls' School where Hilary attended. He is also brother

Notes

of Bishara Awad, head of Bethlehem Bible College, on whose board
I serve.

11. *The Oregonian,* April 14, 1989.

12. Elias Chacour, *Blood Brothers* (Grand Rapids, Mich.: Zonder-
van/Chosen Books, 1984), 146.

13. Chacour, *Blood Brothers,* 168.

14. Shehadeh, *The Third Way,* 36–39.

Appendix

1. Shehadeh, *The Third Way,* 36.